D1002912

Letters from an Observatory

OTHER BOOKS BY SIV CEDERING:

Cup of Cold Water
Letters from the Island
Letters from Helge
Mother Is
How to Eat a Fortune Cookie
The Juggler
Color Poems
The Blue Horse, and Other Night Poems
Twelve Pages from the Floating World
Leken i grishuset
Oxen
Grisen som ville bli ren
Letters from the Floating World, Selected and New Poems
Polis, polis potatisgris
Grisen som ville bli julskinka
Grisen far till Paris
Mannen i ödebyn

TRANSLATIONS BY THE AUTHOR

Det blommande trädet, Native American Poetry
Two Swedish Poets: Gösta Friberg & Göran Palm
You and I and the World: Poems by Werner Aspenström
Pearl's Adventure (translated with David Swickard)

LETTERS FROM AN OBSERVATORY

New and Selected Poems 1973-1998

Siv Cedering

KARMA DOG EDITIONS
Long Island, New York
1998

KARMA DOG EDITIONS

Published by the Karma Dog Design Studio
P.O. Box 42, Ridge, Long Island, New York 11961.

Copyright © 1998 by Siv Cedering

Appreciation is given to the editors of the following publications in which these poems first appeared: *Anteaus, Ancient Mariner, Barnwood, The Black Warrior Review, Bluefish, The Chariton Review, Chicago Review, Confrontation, Cumberland Poetry Review, The East Hampton Star, Fiction International, Focus on Poetry, The Georgia Review, Harper's, Hawaii Literary Review, Kayak, The Kentucky Review, Lake Superior Journal, Luna (Australia), The Massachusetts Review, Mid-American Review, Minnesota Review, Ms., Mundus Artium, Nebo: a literary journal, The New Republic, New Virgina Review, The New York Quarterly, The Paris Review, Partisan Review, Plowshares, Poetry Now, Quarterly Review of Literature, Raccoon, San Marcos Review, Science, Skywriting, Southern Florida Review, Southern Poetry Review, Sumac, The Virginia Quarterly, The Washington Star,* and *Womans' Studies.*

Appreciation is given to the editors of the following anthologies in which these poems first appeared: *The Book of Love,* W.W. Norton, 1998; *The Talking of Hands,* New Rivers Press, 1998; *The Practice of Peace,* Sherman Asher Publications, 1998; *Dog Days,* St. Martin's Press, 1996; *Imagination,* Peconic Gallery, Suffolk Coummunity College, 1992; *Mixed Voices: Contemporary Poems about Music,* Milkweed Editions, 1991; *Long Island Poets,* The Permanent Press, 1986.

The selected poems in this volume have been taken from the following books by the author: *Letters from the Floating World,* University of Pittsburgh Press, 1984; *Color Poems,* Calliopea Press, 1978; *The Juggler,* Sagarin Press, 1977; *Mother Is,* Stein & Day, 1975; *Letters from the Island,* Fiddlehead Books, 1973; *Cup of Cold Water,* New Rivers Press, 1973.

This collection was written with the support of grants from the New York Foundation for the Arts and the Swedish Writers Fund, which are hereby gratefully acknowledged.

International Standard Book Number
0-9631128-5-6

First Edition published September 1998
a   b   c   d   e

Designed by Anthony R. Guilbert

Printed in Canada by
Hignell Printing Limited

for my family

CONTENTS

LETTERS FROM AN OBSERVATORY

I. WHEN THE UNIVERSE BEGAN

II. LISTENING FOR A LARGER SONG

III. THE BOOK OF MONSTERS AND ANGELS

CUP OF COLD WATER

CONTENTS CONTINUED . . .

III. HERBAL

THE JUGGLER

COLOR POEMS

CONTENTS CONTINUED . . .

IV. UKIYO-E: PICTURES OF THE ORDINARY WORLD

V. UKIYO-E: PICTURES OF THE FLOATING WORLD

LETTERS
FROM
AN
OBSERVATORY

The earth is the cradle of the mind, but one cannot
live in a cradle forever.

Konstantin Tsiolkovsky

Can you fasten the harness of the Pleiades, or untie
Orion's belt?
Can you guide the morning star season by season
and show the Bear and its cub which way to go?
Have you grasped the celestial laws?
Could you make their writ run on the earth?

Job 38: 31-33

TURNING

You put your arms around me and I am
part of that larger turning: the earth
in its jet stream, the dancer spinning
around the dark stage, circumscribed
in four-quarter time by the moon.

The way the lights go on and off
in that dark theater
does not matter, or the way matter
transforms, or how vast the space
that even the arms of our galaxy

cannot embrace; for when my skin
listens to the rhythm of your breath,
the voice in the whirlwind
becomes a possibility
and the story still full of beginnings,

so that when your arms unloosen their lock
at midnight and I begin to drift off,
I startle awake for a moment
in the midwinter room and mumble,
"Do you smell it? Spring."

15

CROSSING THE SOUND
ONE NIGHT DURING THE GULF WAR

Leaving the book of love poems beside you,
I go out on deck. Lights of oil refineries
glide by, submarines in dry dock, buoys.
Not able to align the inside with the outside,
I climb the metal stairs for a better view.

In the stern, the frayed flag
snaps the wind and the wake north,
where the Pole Star swings the Cup of the Bear
like a boy betting his little sister
the upside-down bucket won't spill.

No longer believing a star falls
when somebody dies, I still look for the three
in Orion's belt, his sword, the dogs at his feet,
the almost invisible arc of his bow, and follow
his aim past the V-shaped face of the Bull

to the wound. On separate coasts,
my parents are sinking into silence.
A stroke has made it difficult for my brother
to speak. Soon only my sister and I will be left
talking long distance.

Thinking I could slip unheard
over the railing, I lean against the bin
of life jackets, and like a child
who knows the story by heart
I make my way across the heavens,

mouthing the names, "Lyre, Pegasus, Swan,"
while their stories mingle with my own,
my children's. From a plane,
this ferry crossing the Sound
would look like a star falling slowly

from constellation to constellation.
You look up as I enter the lit room.
"I was worried," you say. I touch you
and pick up the book, in which
a man and a woman

learn to love growing old.

WANTING TO KNOW

i.

I want to talk to you
as one talks with hands,
the words as yet unformed
but being shaped
in the space outside.

I want to find the sentence
near your face
as one reaches up to pick the peach
so that its pulp can satisfy
the mouth.

18   Like the bear in the medieval book
gives birth to an unformed cub
to later shape it with her tongue,
I want to begin to bare the phrases
surfacing in my skin.

ii.

Because the fiddlehead fern
unfurls its tight spiral,
and the seed sack of whelk exposes
each miniature shell complete
with its architecture,
and the pebble is polished by the sea
to this amazing shape, or that,

I place my hands on your chest.
If I let my fingers explore
the soft skin at the base of your throat,
the complex muscles of your thighs,
the genitals, predictably changing,
while I question how a being can be contained

in this amazing shape, or that,
will it be because I want to know
that unfurling self,
the architecture of human history,
or what the space is
in Joseph of Armithea's garden,
what the body, what the stone?

iii.
What we know we know,
information tucked
into some sleepy corner
of the brain, where it waits
to be voiced again,
but it is what I don't know
that makes me turn
to you.

Did you, as a child,
have a vision of god,
in that thunderous space
between chaos and
the known world, shaping
the void?
So my fingertips
recall enough

to want to know more,
touch you,
as if there were a void, still,
in Adam's cage,
and our part of creation
is ready to begin,
when the night envelopes us
and light grows
within.

LONG ISLAND WINE

You lift your goblet,
match the color of the liquid
to the color of the sky. "Sauvignon
blanc," you say, as if tasting the words,
then you toast me, take a sip,
and lie down on your back,
looking up.

> The ancient cosmographers
> pictured the sky as an inverted bowl
> containing all of space,
> constant and unchanging –
> except for the predictable dance
> of sun, moon, fixed and
> moving stars.

With a finger I trace
the hand-stitched edge of a patch
on the old quilt we bought
at a roadside stand in Indiana,
where we stopped
for something cool
to drink.

Some woman, born and buried
not far from James Dean,
cut up her faded dress,
the worn slip, the torn skirt,
and stitched them together in a pattern
she called: sun, moon,
and stars.

Underneath the quilt,
the earth drinks
water infused with this indescribable
light, that tugs at seed, sprout, tendril,
the leaf unfolding pale chartreuse,
and the clusters ripening on
the vine.

I stretch out beside you,
feel the faded cloth soft against my skin
and the sweet rush of wine
in my veins, as the sky above us
darkens, from gewürztraminer
to rosé, making water
into wine.

ORBIUM CŒLESTIUM

i. *The Selenographia of Hevelius*

Because you are not here, I read
Kepler, Copernicus, Brahe,
and the other cosmographers
who drew systems they could understand
and defend.

And I wonder why I cannot create
a *philosophiae naturalis* of my own,
believe it totally, and defend it
by myself. Instead
I fantasize,

like Kepler, about a journey to the moon,
a *Somnium*, where you lift me, calm
the confusion of orbits inside me, break
the moon child from her dream.
And then?

Speak to me, write to me.
Any atlas I draw of the heavens
can, like the etching plate Hevelius used
to print his *Selenographia*, be melted
into a copper kettle, a bell, a drum.

ii. *Constellations*

We have shared the same molecules for years
in our lungs, in our blood, in our heart.

If we connected them dot to dot,
the things we know might emerge:

a bed, a table, the geometry of a labyrinth,
a winged creature still looking for its name.

We have not discovered how to connect number
to number; galaxies, molecules move. It is good.

Because what would we do if we saw Adam and Eve
in separate gardens, light-years apart, reaching

23

toward the same sun?

THE BELL COW

The bell cow went first. She had lost her way and come to a tarn one evening. She was thirsty, so she drank. It was autumn. The moon lay like a buttercup on the water. The bell cow drank it.

Then it wasn't long before she wanted to graze in the sky's pasture every night. When evening came, she lifted her head, lowed at the stars, and started to walk. The others followed: white cows walking slowly toward the Milky Way. No one came home for the milking.

Who said the barn door should be closed, that no one should taste the meadow's grass and flowers?

24

10:41 GREENWICH TIME
for Zachariah

Ephraim rose, and a rose opened its pocket watch and checked the time. Minutes matter and seconds accumulate quickly under an Eastern sun. A bird flew against a wall of glass and lay stunned, while its heart beat the insistence of sky. A breath of wind that had been hiding in a stand of bulrushes slid through the whispering reeds, to rise just in time to clear the wave that fell back from its first push against the shore. The tide rang its school-bell, and like obedient children, each drop of current got in line. In a city, not far away, a hand lifted a pen to record the dead, while a boy balanced on a wall, and a girl played hopscotch without breaking her mother's back. A letter of no particular importance was written, one was delivered, yet another one read, while on another continent, a woman's belly was slit and an infant was lifted up to open its eyelids uncertainly and see the light of the day for the first time.

25

BECAUSE THE DOG DEMANDS

I leave the lamplit lane
and walk into the dark.
I cannot detect the scent
of pheasant, fox,
the doe who lost her way,
or the creature that screeched
the copulating cry
that woke me in the night,
but he pulls me on
past subtleties as refined,
perhaps, as Botticelli or Boccherini
to a canine mind.

When I turn to go back,
he does his dance in the tall grass
and squats on trembling legs,
as vulnerable to the world
– and intent on doing –
as any human being.
At the end of the leash,
I tilt my head back, looking up.
Only a bit of information
separates the stars in their patterns
from the fireflies that float
in the dark, mating.

The woman you went to see
and the man I carried
like a stone in my gut
are almost forgotten.
Through tangles of bittersweet,
I see the light from our porch
and the windows lit up,
waiting.

THE PROCESSION
for Ellen Frank

You touch my shoulder. I turn my head.
You ask about the procession,
You ask about my hands,
the vessel for the child,
the amphora.

All day I have walked from Alexandria.
What Hyptia did has everything
to do with the stars
and the stretching of space
that pulls the song out of the singer.

It does not matter if we try
to explain it with notes, color,
or geometrical shapes.
I reach out and touch Futura.
She turns her head, takes my hand,

but continues leading.
Of course we follow each other.
Of course we carry what we love.
Of course the gesture turns into
a libation.

It is not a matter of sacrifice
but celebration,
of being part of
what makes the new moon
rise from the horn of the ram.

RECORDING AT THE AUTUMN EQUINOX

The black body of a heron flies
across the last rose
of the sky
to light
near the black grass of the shore,
the splash almost inaudible. You say, "Too beautiful,"

What is that drone? You shake your head
and rub your ear like the mutt at your feet
to undo the eardrum's trembling. "Too loud to be a plane,"
you say, yet you look up and watch an emerald light
crossing the darkening green sky
toward Providence.

The sounds resound, whether or not
the soles of our neighbor's feet tap a muted beat
against the wooden planks of the dock
or the motor of his boat purrs
in higher and higher gear
as man and boat melt into a silhouette

that moves across the water,
while the crickets on the shore wind down.
Is it the dark that amplifies the sounds?
Is someone really beating a kettle drum,
or is that loud druming just a boy
hitting a stick against a buoy

on the other side of the harbor, three miles away?
While we listen, the stars come out.
You crane your neck to watch the white strobe of a jet
heading toward Europe, and way up high, so slow
it barely seems to be moving – a speck of light.
Surveillance plane? Satellite?

This country is not at war. We can sit quite peacefully
on shore and talk of brown tide, red tide, of changing
diapers on the old. It's daylight, still, somewhere.
The sun never sets on the Air Force
and war games perpetually played
by computers simulating God,

while politicians turn in their sleep,
where missiles are made from money
saved for milk and an apple a day.
We watch the light from the lighthouse
flick on, and off, and on.
"I'll do the dishes," you say and go inside.

This is a recording. It began at the sound
of the first bird at first light
and is still running.
I am listening for the message, to learn what that drone is
and where the wolf is, when the sound is at the door
and everything is, as you say, "too beautiful, "

MEMORIAL DAY

Two by two,
the horseshoe crabs
ease across
the shallows.

The loops and lines
their bodies make
can be seen
at low tide.

Oblivious
to what propels them
to this calligraphy
of procreation,

two old crustaceans,
crusted with barnacles,
stop at the water's edge
attached.

In the village,
the American flags
flap their messages
furiously

to vacationers,
shoppers, bikers
who pump their tires
for the first time this season.

While you and I
steal the afternoon
from all that should be done
and remembered

and, with our bodies
still coupled,
fall asleep
forgetting everything.

SUNDAY THEORIES

When parts of the paper are strewn
around the room, and the discounted fares
have made you think of walking down
a street in Rome, when the puzzle is
abandoned, the *Book Review*, and the two
of you have talked of buying tickets
to "Winterreise," you push the tray aside
– never mind the crumbs – to define
your bodies on the bed,
as late morning turns

to early afternoon. When sleep
catches one of you unaware,
the other might absent-mindedly observe
the curve of an eyebrow, or the star-
burst beside the eye, and think
that every eyelash of that familiar face,
seeming so still, is composed
of moving particles that began to spin
when the universe began.
And as you stretch, shift your gaze

to some other feature of that face,
you might think it conceivable
that the proof of the Unified Field Theory
could be found in such a place.

But before you can compare
the saddle-shape of hips and waist
to some model of the universe,
the dog scratches at the door.
You sigh, get up and let him in,
and return to see the sleeper turn

– and reveal the white at the temple.
And while you consider the relationship
of light to the fifth dimension, the sleeper
wakes. And because the day is lovely
and the slanting autumn light
brings all the colors of the ancient elements
into play, you leave the bed in disarray,
get dressed and go outside, where
– as a proof of the fourth dimension –
you comment on a falling leaf.

THE POEM I AM NOT WRITING

This is the poem I am not writing,
the one in which I am wordless
but looking for the right word,
searching further and further back
for meaning. It is not a dream.
I do not wake up mouthing it,
tucked between the tip of my tongue
and parting lips. Somewhere
in the back of my brain, it flickers.
A root lights up for a moment
and flashes on its many cousins,
more or less foreign, a syllable
that has been muttered, maybe,
by an old hag in Old England,
or spelled by a monk, trying to write
in Latin, hoping God understands
at least one language.

People travel around the world to explore
and die for more than one reason.
What is the relationship between mute
and moder, mother, mutter, matter?
between Mamma and mammary
in the far reaches of memory?
I placed my infant hands
around the soft, warm globes
and repeated, nenne,
while the soothing cascades of
my mother's words
began to set the muscles of my cheeks,
my face, so that her way of speaking
would leave a tone in every syllable

I would pronounce, in whatever language,
and pull me back to explore
the still uncharted regions of Terra Incognita.

Not every search is a search for god,
but if the word is god, the root
might have been cooed by an infant,
as she squirmed with sweet milk and
satisfaction, gheu,
while looking at her mother,
who smiled in recognition
and repeated her way of saying
god, gud, without questioning
how both mother and child,
can be a divinity to the other
and how that seed of sanction
set the lips to utter
a sentence in whatever tongue,
beginning with that cry of existence,
I – jag, je, yo, ik, ich, mino, mi –
while fumbling for a word like love.

MY DICTIONARY

The volume where I search for meaning
is well-worn, the first fifty some pages
gone. The new first begins
with artificial horizon and ends
before the end with Asclepius,
the Greek god of the healing art.
At night, I listen to my heart.
At night, when the light is out
I question the lump, imagined or not,
in my flesh, my throat,
and what the pain really is, and when
it will come again.
Artisan, artist, artiste, I read.
The differentiations are slight

but paramount. Artistic, artistry,
and artless also considers
art, or the lack of it, like arty does.
Then arum, having the flowers
of a fleshy spike subtended by
a leafy bract. The genus includes
the cuckoopint and any of several related
plants, as the jack-in-the-pulpit.
From that green flasher of the woods, I turn
to arundinaceous: of, pertaining to,
or like a reed – and read on.
The various forms of ascending
leads to ascent, act of rising; rise.
Advancement in status or esteem.

A going up, as the ascent of Mont Blanc.
The metaphors are free.
An upward slope; acclivity.
I repeat acclivity aloud.
What exactly does it mean?
That section of the book is gone.
I go on to ascertain, to find out
or learn for a certainty,
by trial, examination or experiment;
to get to know. And so I go
to ascetic. Given to strict self-denial,
especially (abbreviated esp.)
for the sake of spiritual or intellectual
discipline. There I stop.
What was the word I wanted to look up?

TWO STANZAS

The word stanza means room, I repeat
and sigh, of course, as if I finally
understand. Like my mother and father
reworked blueprints
on summer Sundays on the island,
while my sister and I drew house plans
with sticks in the red sand,
I try to shape this stanza –

and the next, rectangle by rectangle.
Erase a line and a wall disappears.
Move a window for a better view.
And if I am uncertain of
the final version,
I remember the swimming lesson –
and keep moving my arms and legs,
confident that my father's hand
is under my belly
even when he lets go.

THE PLACE MY WORDS ARE
LOOKING FOR

Suppose I were as clever as a bird
and the words for what I am
could be contained
in one precise song,
repeated, repeated
while each jubilant phrase
spells it all
in variations
too refined for the human ear.

Or that the song has not yet been found
but waits inside me
like the long note that sounds
when a blade of grass
is placed between the thumbs
and blown.

It could be
that the place my words are looking for
will turn out to be so small
that there will be room for nothing
but silence –
or an ocean so large
some waves will never reach
the sound of the shore.

WAITING FOR THE STORY

Not far from the side of a red barn and
a pond ringed with tall reeds and grasses,
cattails, maybe, rushes, lythrum or fireweed
– something magenta,

blue sticks of dragonflies hovered
on iridescent wings, making me think of
my grandfather and grandmother
meeting in such a place
the year before my father was born,

and of my father moving through a field,
not unlike the one on the other side of the road,
his scythe swinging, while the wild flowers
on the summer dress of the woman
who would be my mother
fell to the ground.

Sometimes it takes a long time
for an image to tell its story.
The red barn and the blooming magenta spikes
might have nothing to do with my family,
and dragonflies mating on the wing
above their perfect reflections
might have nothing to do with love.

RIDING A BREAKER

This is not about the porpoise
stranded near the bulkhead
or the dark sail of its flipper
holding its course in the wind,
or the red tear of blood
dripping from an eye,
or the mouth left open.

This is not about the water
where that porpoise used to turn
on the rotating wheel of its ride,
chattering in high-pitched sonar
or piping a song.
It is not even about what it was
that forced it out of its element.

This is not about numbers,
although we point to them as if
they could anchor our existence.
"In March it will be ten years!"
you shout from the crest
of a wave, waving,
while the sunset leaves

the ocean burning.
Time is measured by this turning.
"It is getting dark," I call,
a taste of salt water in my mouth,
and ride a breaker ashore,
knowing we must continue
counting and accounting.

VARIATIONS FOR THE PIANO

i.
On El Camino Del Mar
in San Francisco,
I stopped outside a white façade
to hear the notes of a sonata
spill through the ornate wrought-iron railing
of a narrow Spanish verandah.

Still a Match Girl at fifteen,
I stood in the dark Pacific air,
as the moon lit a white blossom
on each black leaf of
a gardenia.

ii.
When the moon has gone, past Sardinia,
I stand outside an Italian villa,
hearing the perfect notes of a sonatina
spilling over the verandah.

Grateful for the vision
(Oh, the vision!)
I have burned all my matches
to stand here in the dark
seeing the black water of the bay
catch the white reflection
of a street light on the quay
in each undulation.

iii.
Once a man from Bowling Green, Ohio
(or was it Bloomington, Indiana?)

laughed out loud at the idea
of a child by the Arctic Circle
playing the piano.

And somewhere in that mythic Thule,
I stared at a postcard
a pen-pal sent from Manitoba.
Unable to comprehend
that one could live in such desolation,
I turned back to the piano
to follow the ascending black notes
of Schumann's "Träumerei,"
loving the hesitant, changing note
          (the eighth in the melody
          of each variation)

          iv.
No longer believing that Ultima Thule
is in some foreign country,
I stop by the Bay of Napoli,
listening to someone practice
the piano
– and almost laugh out loud
          (pianissimo, pianissimo)
at the sweet irony
of trying to learn the finale,
while someone else is striking the keys,
keeping the tempo
on black and white
ebony, ivory.

SEEING A PHOTOGRAPH: A SENTENCE

Seeing a black and white photograph of
the striped interior of a cathedral,
I think of the great northern diver,
the common loon, the loom,
brilliant in contrast in summer plumage,

and I wonder if the creator of such a structure,
planning the bold layers
or fitting the stripes around some extremity
of shape – arc or dome – heavy yet climbing
toward his vision of heaven,

thought of the human skeleton,
the white ribs that cage the dark space
of breath, while days and nights
leave their light and dark impressions
inside us,

not fossilized in flesh or banded in bone,
like rings in the trunk of a tree,
but layered in an indefinable place,
retrievable, like the sound of
the voice in the dark audience asking,

"How do we imagine, and speak of,
the void?" while on the brightly-lit stage
someone asks how we imagine, and speak of,
our own death – or simply that we are,
then we are not,

like the loner bird
or the interior of
a cathedral.

44

NUDE DESCENDING: A ROUND

The dark shape
descending
makes me turn my head
away from the green
luminescent
screen,

rise,
run down-
stairs naked to
see the great blue
heron
light,

turn its head
to see
the shape of my
light
body
descending,
rise.

EMILY'S MINUET

There is a darkness in the lightest room
I cannot light.
I face it when I avert my face.
I cannot do without

it. Alternately white and black
its shade burns my neck
when I turn to face the light.
A white stone dropped in the darkest water

is no less
than this dark stone,
rising in the bright room of the heart.

TABLE MANNERS

I have tried to place the forks and knives of my life
and the glass with its bulb of light, just right.
I have ladled a portion of praise on the plate of each child
and made the helping big, so the man beside me
could sleep content with his labor.

But setting the table does not satisfy
the voracious one. Never content with scraps,
he demands more than Elijah's share.
Not cowering, not begging, he sits back while I clear.

There are reasons why animals go for the heart
or that other organ named for life.
"Down, down," I say. "Wait," and the large, white bird
in my harbor takes flight, the machinery of
wings and air complaining.

Oh, I have set the table. I have filled the glass
like a chemist. I have moved the mass
from container to container
but have found no vessel spacious enough to hold
the course of this feast.

If you happen to enter, to sit at my table, consider
how you hold the glass where the world seems
containable. And as you cut your portion,
help me phrase the inverted song
of the reflected one in the spoon.

CALLING YOU ISHMAEL

"Call me Ahab,"
you say the night
before going on
board, and
I am scared,
for both of us
know that dark

captain. The day
brightens. The vessel
one we
take in hope
of seeing some larger
being. There
she blows,

and there,
a pair, flipper
and fluke splash, half-
dark, half-light
a tail breaks
the surface so
near, beyond

reach. The humpbacks
breach!
Not sure I can remain
in my body, I face

your face. Leaping
with such unexpected
grace might have a reason

more definable than
joy, something explained
biologically, yet
this enthusiasm reminds me
the word is
rooted in the spirit
of god.

Standing near
you, I ask: why
Ahab?
The catch is the catch.
The pursuit goes on
for the light
Leviathan.

And he alone remains
who tells the tale
beginning – before
embarking on that white
chapter – by
asking to be called
another name.

COUNTRY MUSIC

You say you like whales, and I surface, spout
toward the heavens, flip my tail and listen
for your strange song. "Beluga – Beluga!"
I wallow in delight with everything that's large
about me, wanting to be larger beside you,
to tumble, touched everywhere, as if by water,
the waves billowing from such leviathan playing.

You say you love flamenco dancers, and
my swayed back arches, my waist grows slender,
my buttocks firm, and nothing is hidden
in the tight red dress that flares like a fuchsia
around my insistently stamping feet: "Now! Now!"
– the quickening heartbeat of my petulant desire.
My head is high, my eyes cast behind the fan
that opens and closes my face to entice you.

You say you wanted to marry a Chippewa princess
when you were eight, and I tell about the doeskin
dress I bought from a trader in a motel room
in Colorado. Its bleached skins are soft,
fringed, the bead work complex. It waits
in my attic. I have not felt I have the right
to wear it, but now I want to put it on and go
to the mountain where you want to marry me.

Oh, middle age is sweet. I can with confidence say
I know almost as much about love as I did
when I was seven and serenaded a beautiful
blue-eyed boy from under his balcony, while dancing
the hula under the midnight sun of the Arctic.
Yes, I knew about love. I knew what to do.
You laugh. We laugh, rolling in the billow of
the bed, to poise ourselves in that formal dance,

before we are done and sink into the sigh
of a promise as true as the one we have made
to the land. Not having found the language yet
for everything that opens inside me,
I speak of the internal loaves and fishes
that divide themselves like cells, the thousand hands
that reach for you, the thousand eyes that see you
in each unfolding miracle of this world.

For I would go westward with you, riding
on one horse, if we had only one, or walking,
if we had none. Meanwhile, I part my hair
in the back and braid two even braids. I cultivate
the perfect rose, not knowing when
I might need to bite the stem, to quench the scream.
I swim out beyond the crashing breakers and dive deep
into the flickering light, listening for a larger song.

GOAT SESTINA

"El Sueño de la Razón Produce Monstruos"
Francisco Goya

"The Sleep of Reason Produces Monsters,"
you say aloud, reading the titles of
Francisco Goya's Caprichos
in a newspaper article on war.
The word caprichos lingers in my mind
and begins to unravel its history.

I don't know much about the history
of words, or how monsters,
or angels, breed in the mind,
or why Goya chose a word full of
tricks for his pictures of internal war
and human folly, or why caprice and capers

suddenly have new meaning. Kids,
our President said on TV, making history,
when speaking of soldiers fighting a war
with the word for goat-child, while the monsters
of our arsenals were paraded as a sign of
strength, baffling my mind.

Watching the news, my mind
switches to Capri, where, over insalata caprese,
you said the word for goat was also at the root of
tragedy and we should let history
help us predict that monsters
will, again, be released by war.

There is no such thing as a war
out there. Everything is internal. The mind

is all it knows. Monsters
stir in our sleep. The unnamed capriped
climbs the crags of history,

leaving the prophesied mark of
the beast in my heart. I want to speak of
love, but the word war
has invaded my personal history.
Whatever path I choose in my mind,
I confront the Goat-footed One
and face myself, the two-headed monster.

I wish I could think of a word to ease the mind,
as I paint this war. The sun is in Capricorn.
The book of history lies open to a page of monsters.

53

TV NEWS FROM THE GULF:
A VILLANELLE

The picture as presented is quite clear
The sky is blue. The day is bright.
Not propelled by wings, the bird comes near.

The sound of small waves lapping please the ear.
Reflected sunlight makes the waters light.
The picture as presented is quite clear.

We see the head of a loon-like bird disappear
In an undulation that looks almost white.
Not propelled by wings, the bird comes near,

Shaking its head. Neither sea water nor tear,
The liquid clings, black as night.
The picture as presented is quite clear.

The bird is a cormorant. Its feathers, we hear,
Look like a starry sky. It walks upright.
Not propelled by wings, the bird comes near

And stumbles. With fear
We watch the fall. A prophecy takes flight.
The picture as presented is quite clear.
Not propelled by wings, the bird comes near.

YOUR SNAKES

You coddled them, tucked them away,
ignored the fact that they wanted out.
It became a habit to keep the lid shut.
You did not expect them to proliferate
in the dark. You did not think of them
at all. Why should you? We are living
in modern times. Old stories are just

metaphors. But one day,
something irrelevant reminds you,
when you are traveling down the road, say,
twisting the dial from radio evangelist
to blue grass. And the lock snaps open,
as it must. The lid lifts.
And you look inside the box.

How intricate the geometrics
on their backs. How delicate
the flicking of their tongues.
Of course, they can circle your fingers,
bracelet your wrist. You straighten
your arm and admire the result.
And you let a snake slither

down between your breasts.
You do not stop the one that slides
up your legs. You help the three
that are braiding themselves
into your hair. And a snake slips
out of your mouth. The pain eases.
Wherever you are traveling,
you notice the landscape.
It looks just right for snakes.

SKIMMING THE SURFACE

I sweep a light skimmer across the dark pool
and whisk out a wet-whiskered mole,
a hole-mouse, a sleek slip of fur.

I should be glad to be rid of this fat-bellied cousin
of vole and rat, to put an end to its insistent digging,
to stop the invisible nibbling up of bulb and root
by at least one subversive subterranean.

I should feel justified in tossing out
the plump burrower, uninvited borrower of land I call mine,
this undermining mound-builder who has left my lawn
as rippled with ridges as faille or gabardine.

I should, perhaps, have listened to those
who gave lengthy lessons over wine at garden parties
on how to set a trap in every mole-made skylight
or plop a camphor ball into each mini-mineshaft

so the gas could fill the subways and chase
the tiny tunneler out, or kill. But
like a burrowing fool, I close my eyes to reason.
I try to remember that not everything

is a reminder of something human.
Things can be just things, acts simply acts,
and your way of finding the moist shaft
where you can burrow, pushing that blind head

toward a sensing of eternity should not make
every creature I find a porter of parables, or
evoke the Orphic journey into that dark underground
or provoke the question of

what kind of singing could bring a beloved back.
Still I place the small body down on the other side
of the fence, so the dead creature won't be a toy
for a dog – or a plaything for a beast who is human.

THE MONKEY'S CHILDREN

Here is a story for you.
The monkey had two children.
She loved the fair one
and cuddled it close to her breast.
She hated the dark one,
who persistently clung to her back.
When the hunters came
and she escaped up a tree,
the fair one fell to the ground,
while the dark brat held on.

I don't know what you do
with the monkey on your back.
I talk to mine and pass him
coriander seeds and fruit.
I have come to like his tug
at my back. Even when the fair one
is awake, a sweet weight in my arms,
I slip my hand around my waist
to feel the other one's touch.

The other day when the hunters came,
and I scurried to the highest branch,
the fair one slipped out of my grasp.
The dark one flung out a bare-knuckled fist
and caught my love in the air.

PASIPHAE'S CLAIM

Let them whisper behind my back
about the hair, the tail of the beast.
Let them construct labyrinths
and pray he will lose his way.
Let them curse his father
and keep their daughters
out of his sight.
He will claim what is his.

I do not disown him.
Even if I had known
what that unsanctioned union
would bring,
I would have locked my thighs
around that alban mount.

I know my skin is white.
I know my mind –
and that every monster
is conceived in thought.
So how could I not love this being,
part animal, part man, part of
what I am?

59

SMALL TOWN CIRCUS

So when the muscle man at the circus
said he was the strongest man,
I said, "No stronger than my father."
And when he claimed to be the heaviest man,
I said, "Yeah, with lead in your boots."

Of course, I trembled
at the anger in his eyes that said
he ought to squash the snot-nose,
but the town was small and I knew
the freaks were no different from us.

A MAN CALLED DEATH

Of course, I believed he was there,
as they said, walking
the roads after dark, alone,
and that I would recognized him
from the white cross on the back
of his black leather coat,
and that, if I saw him face to face,
he would say, "I am death,"
which would mean I would die.

Of course, I believe he is here,
somewhere in my neighborhood,
and that I might meet him,
say, while walking the dog,
but I have not as yet seen his face.
I don't even know if he has a face
or what sign he might see on my back,
if he approaches from the back,
or what, on facing him, I will say.

ANGEL SESTINA

My mother never said that she had seen the angel
standing by the headboard of her bed,
or that she believed it would always
guard the sleeping child,
or that it would remain until morning
content to be watching, waiting.

She never said she lay awake during the night, waiting
for her own mother's neglectful angel
to return to its place before morning,
when she, a girl of thirteen, would run to her mother's bed
as eager as any child
to see if her mother was there, as always.

She never told me to distrust the word always
or said what it is like to learn that the waiting
creature by the bed is neither the kind a child
remembers from Sunday school, nor the feared angel
of judgment, but a scrawny creature hovering by the bed,
to peck at the falling feathers of morning.

She did not spell out what she did, the first morning
her own mother could not rise, as always,
or what they discussed, as her mother stayed in bed
unable to tend to the chores waiting,
or when exactly the two of them realized that the angel
protects neither mother nor child.

She did not teach her own child
to mistrust the dark or to pray for morning.
She did not warn me that the angel
would change, that a darker one would always
appear, to crouch on the headboard, waiting,
growing gaunt and contorted like the woman in the bed.

She did not say I would stand by her bed,
suddenly no longer a child,
praying the hunched creature waiting
will be patient, at least until morning,
before it devours the word always
and, from my mother's contorted body, rips the angel.

Back in my own bed, I sort the feathers of morning.
Like any child who has been forced to trade always
for never, I glance over my shoulder, waiting for the angel.

SEA-DRIFT

On the first warm day, when both the front door
and the storm door are left casually ajar
without thought of conserving fuel,
and the storm windows on the south wall
are taken down, and the Windex is out,
and a pile of old newspapers is waiting
on the stoop, and the chickadees
are scattering the odor of sun-warmed pine,
you take the folded aluminum chair
that has hung on a nail all winter long,
and walk down the cement block stairs
to the strip of sand
that spans the narrow slope
between ebb and tide.

You unbutton your blouse at the neck,
roll up the sleeves, notice a blue heron light
on the mud flat – and that quick, white flitting
with the sharp cry must be the shy
roseate tern already back!
You adjust your chair,
brush away a strand of hair,
pull up your skirt so the thin, white skin
of your knees can feel the sun.
In the shallows,
diagonal lines of light knot their flickering nets
over scallop shells, razor clams,
the absurd scuttling of an old crab.
What did you say, once upon a time,

about swimming out into the cold,
when you grew old,
beyond the surf, to grow numb, overcome
by some benign fatigue, to simply sink
in the sea-drift, a gentle accident, well-planned,
executed while you still could use your will,
so not to end tied to a wheel-chair
in a nursing home, half-blind,
or in a hospital bed,
hooked to a tangle of tubes?
You untie your shoes and place them neatly,
side by side, beside the chair, take off
your socks and roll them up into a ball,
thinking the swallows will soon be back

under the eaves, and the beach-plums
will bloom, and the wild roses on the dune.
The sand feels warm under your bare feet.
Even the water in the shallows
is warmed by the sun.
Minnows scatter as you step in,
laughing, feeling like a child
on the first day of summer,
before knowing how to swim,
standing with a new bucket and a shovel,
ready for the splashing to begin,
while the still nameless birds
announce their return
with their crying, their song.

AFTER THE ACCIDENT

While trying to control my hands
enough to print the names and numbers
of license and insurance card,
I hear the dogs of Odin bark.

and look up. They omen death.

But way above the scattering
of broken glass and twisted steel,
the wild geese
are reshaping their V's.

66

AVIARY

This island is not an aviary,
although the air is spring-full of wings.

The singing is just a confirmation,
as is the single feather found on the beach.

The fact that I ask you to rub the ache in my shoulder
                                        blades
might be because of what I have been planting,

or age, and not any Icarian escape.
But sometimes I am Daedaleus, seeing a part of myself

climb higher, freed by air flow,
at the same time as I am that son, suspended, looking
                                        down,

thinking the older self can not quite hide
the flight of fear across the face,

– then the parent, again, watching the plumage break
                                        apart
and the plummeting. And yet

I let myself take off, to soar sun-high, sea-bound,
the quills quivering.

THE BOOK OF MONSTERS AND ANGELS

If the sea gull were a rare bird, a sighting
would be considered an omen. Men would tell
and retell how that harbinger of peace, or war, came
and forced them to listen. Women would whisper
about the apparition they accepted as an annunciation
and point to the arc of the wing and the markings
confirming the vision. Not only a shaman
would keep a foot as a relic, a feather as a talisman.
The mark of a beak could lead to hours of
                                        fortune telling.
Amazed, we would try to fathom how the winged
                                        creature
could endure for thousands of miles in the wake
of a ship – or return every day to drop a clam
on our rock. With muted voices we would question
what the cries mean, sounding so human.

If a human being were a rare creature, the book of
monsters and angels would define the wonder.
Not needing to mention the good or evil
we are capable of, the world's newspapers would,
like parents of their firstborn, announce

the miracle of each step, each word.
As museums opened and closed their doors
on yet another aspect of the human,
there would be lectures on the ability to see,
the mystery of perception – and discussions
on how an image can be held in the mind,
embodied in a word, expressed in sound,
that can be captured in letters that then
can be pronounced, again, conveying that vision.

On this coast, the swan is quite common
and often a nuisance in parks. Its neck
is disproportionately long, its walk
awkward, and the cob too aggressive
for a child bringing bread. Even the pair
we awaited took off in graceless flight
on wings that sounded like hinges squeaking.
But seeing the two glide toward our shore
makes me mouth the word visitation.
And as the setting sun blazes along the curve of a wing
and ignites a glow deep in the spreading feathers,
I am Leda burying my fingers in celestial plumage,
holding on, as if proof of the flight
will be spelled out in the night constellation.

1973
Poems
Selected
From :

CUP
OF
COLD
WATER

I light the stove
in the empty house;
a fly awakens.

I laugh at myself.

I had come to be alone.

CUP OF COLD WATER

i.

I scoop a bucket
full of snow,

heap the whiteness
in a bowl
and set it by the stove,

that we can wash
our hands.

I fill the bucket
full again

to melt:
a small amount

for us
to drink.

ii.

When we have slept
the measure of the night,

we wash our hands
break the bread
and lift our cups.
You say:

this water lacks
the journey through the earth,
the taste of soil
and rock.

It has traveled
only through the air.
What good is heaven
in a lover's cup?

iii.
The snow is coming down.

We open the door
to look
and let the cold
come in.

I say: In summer
when the snow is rain,
I will put the bucket out
and fill it full
that I can wash my hair
with rain.

You cup my face.
You say:

iv.

In the spring I bend to drink.
The brook is full of melting things.

My two hands form a broken cup
to hold the taste of
granite, moss,
a trace of
rabbit, grouse.

I cup my hands to drink again
– water falls
full of hooves
of moose and deer.
The vessel of my fingers spills

the print of weasel and of quail,
and as sun breaks over rock,
mountains melt and river
in my mouth.

POMEGRANATES

you take me to the woods
where the sun is still warm
on brown leaves
you show me how to squeeze
the fruit
bite a small hole
and suck

fresh water sifted in soil
drawn by roots to rise
in the trunk
to be red and sweet
in the fruit
and yet sweeter
in my mouth
before I give you
to drink

ORNITHOLOGY

The woodcock rises
in a complicated dance.
The cardinal has color.
The lark has song.
And some small birds
attract their mates
with intricate
constructions.

I brush my hair,
wear bright colors and
French perfume,
and walk around my garden,

kick a pebble and
pick a rose,
lift the rose up
to my lips
to feel a petal:
penis skin.

ICE

While we were sleeping
the ice came.

It covered each branch,
roof,
walk,

and every blade of grass
had its own icicle
growing upward
from the lawn.

I sucked the ice
on the tips of branches.

I slipped my gloved fingers
over fences, pines,
the thickened shapes
of leaves.

And I showed my guests
these gardens.

A branch broke,
and another.

A tree snapped,
and
another.

What could we do –
spend the night, outside,
holding up those old
lilacs?

Or, with a candle,
try to melt the space around
each petrified
bud?

And we fell asleep
thinking of ice
around clocks,
still ticking,

ice in the shape of cups
and covering
tables . . .

and us, in our beds:
sheets and flowering
pillowcases,

how perfectly the ice
would curve
around nostrils
and half-parted lips,

the exposed breast, ice nipple,
hair held in its
flowing,

genitals in that
transparent
cold,

and our fingers,
holding our sleep,
frozen like the tips
of branches.

WHITE AND THE RIVER

i.

I am my father.

I go out into the whiteness.
My skis slide their parallel
lines,
and poles alternate
their star prints.

I go to hunt some white thing,
some ptarmigan that lost all color
for this season,
I will hunt her home,
hang her by her feet in the cellar,
where she can spread
her white wings,
while I pull her snow feathers
off
for the dark roast
she will become
on the white cloth
of my Sunday table,

– or some ermine,

regal white weasel
with the black tail tip,
I will catch
and kill,

strip the skin off
to reveal the smell.

Kings and queens
are little girl dreams.

– or a hare
will leap
shot.

ii.
And I am my brother.
I walk with my father
by the river.

We shall cross the river.
We know the ice is
thin.

I say:
"If you fall in
I will let you drown.

I will not pull you up.
I will push you
in."

And he looks at me,
and we walk, together,
out on the ice

that cracks,
but holds,
and cracks.

If he fell in,
would he swim
underneath the ice,

groping for a place
where he would find
a breath,

and another,
to surface someplace,
further down river

where the current is harder
and ice cannot hold,
to return,

would he return
to swim in my dream?
– or sink

and lie on the bottom
as I lay
when I was four

and the boat had tipped over,
and my father found me
on the bottom of the river

and pulled me up
so that I can say:
"If you fall in
I will let you drown."

iii.
And I am my father,
and the boat has tipped over.

I dive for my son
again and
again,

until I see him lying
on the bottom of the river,
arms straight out
and eyes
looking up,

and I dive to his blue eyes
and pull the small body

through water to surface
air and
shore.

     iv.
And I am my mother,
I wash by the
river.

Boil the sheets
white,
and scrub at the
rugs.

The sun is warm.
It is good by
the river.

Rinse the clothes
clean
to blow dry
in the wind.

And my daughters call me.
"Run. Mamma.
Run.

The horse has kicked
brother. The hoof in his
face."

The hoof in his face
while I wash by
the river.

The hoof in his face.

The hoof in his face.

v.

Daughter, sister,
girl who picked
flowers,

(I wear a scar
on my face from
the hoof.)

marsh marigold,
the first by
the river,

      Why did you set
      the furniture
      on fire?"

and bunches of violets
brought home to
mother.

      Why did you lose
      the nails and
      the screws?"

I lifted the skulls of
cows and
oxen

observing
that flowers grow
wilder

where bones
had been thrown
from the butchery shop.

vi.
And I am my father,
and I stop,
pull an orange from my pocket
and peel it,
throw the peelings on the snow,

pick up my gun
and ski back home,
hang my white killing
on a hook in the cellar
where blood oranges lie

a crateful
of color
in winter.

FIGURE EIGHTS

My back toward the circle, I skate,
shift my weight, turn toward the center.

The skill is in the balance, the ability
to choose an edge, and let it cut

its smooth line. The moon is trapped
in the ice. My body flows

across it. The evening's cold. The space
limited. There is not much room

for hesitation. But I have learned a lot
about grace, in my thirty-third year.

I lean into the cutting edge: two circles
interlock, number eight drawn

by a child, a mathematician's
infinity.

THERE IS A GAME WE USED TO PLAY

I take your hand: the fish is caught, scratch a circle around
your wrist: the head is cut. One of my nails draws a line
up your inner arm: the belly's slit. All my fingers flutter
near that slit: the intestines come out. One of my fingers
is a knife that scrapes, quick and hard, until all scales are
off. Then my hands stroke the skin of your arm, up and
down: water, rinsing. The fish is clean. Pat some butter
on, sprinkle salt. Pepper, parsley. Put your arm, then, in
the fire. Let it cook.

I take the fingers of the other hand (there is a game) chop
the head off (we used to play) slit the belly, throw the
intestines to the dog (to please our senses) rinse you clean,
prepare you for the fire.   87

RESCUE, A LETTER

i.

I cannot move my feet.
They are covered with blankets.
My feet are a hospital.
The people who crashed in the sea
are rescued and brought
to my feet.
I am told not to move them.
The beds would tumble
and blood banks.
Nurses. Doctors. Sirens.
Corridors.

ii.

I sit in bed.
I want to read your poems,
slowly, one by one,
but my son
creates an airport and
a sea. Planes
crash. SOS. Rescue
mission. Radios. Messages punctuated:
"Mamma, look!"

I guess I could have chosen
a more quiet place,
if I could choose.
But I accept
the small god in this child.
He knows no death. The pillow
is a shore. He numbers planes
and rescue cars. All vehicles
and men
get home.

iii.

It is morning, last day of March,
I write you this:
I am rescued, every day, from
nothingness. On paper after paper
my left-handed son
creates a body, head,
long hair, eyes, nose and
smile. Just this week
the circle of my body was centered:
navel. I sometimes stand beside a house
that has a door that opens
to an upstairs room. Above the roof,
the cross of a plane
hesitates.

I have no fingers, but my arms
are straight and always
reaching
up. I seem to wait for the day
when some god
will give me
hands. You – from what ocean
would you rescue me, on the day
when wings break and breakers wash
the wings? And when you create
my body on a page, how would you
center me – and give my reaching arms
hands?

HANDS

i.
When I fall asleep
my hands leave me.

They pick up pens
and draw creatures
with five feathers
on each wing.

The creatures multiply.
They say: "We are large
like your father's
hands."

They say: "We
have your mother's
knuckles."

I speak to them:
"If you are hands,
why don't you
touch?"

And the wings beat
the air, clapping.
They fly

high above elbows
and wrists.
They open windows
and leave

rooms.
They perch in treetops
and hide under bushes
biting

their nails. "Hands,"
I call them.
But it is fall

and all creatures
with wings
prepare to fly
south.

      ii.
When I sleep
the shadows of my hands
come to me.

They are softer than feathers
and warm as creatures
who have been close
to the sun.

They say: "We are the giver,"
and tell of oranges
growing on trees.

They say: "We are the vessel,"
and tell of journeys
through water.

They say: "We are the cup."

And I stir in my sleep.
Hands pull triggers
and cut
trees. But

the shadows of my hands
tuck their heads
under wings
waiting

for morning,
when I will wake
braiding

three strands of hair
into one.

THE HORSES

The horses that wake me
walk slowly
straining their long loads,

and something of death and
my father
pulls me to see again

grandfather's mare and
the sled,
heavy up the hill in snow,

pulling an infant brother
to burial
on the mountain.

In my father's workshop
there was
an orange can of glue

with two horses perpetually
pulling
in opposite directions –

something I stared at
to understand.
They are working horses,

and they keep pulling.

NAUTILUS

i.
And here
again:
the slice of chambered nautilus,

the absolutely
perfect
spiral, my simple mathematics

cannot
comprehend:
(logarithmic? exponential?)

but I hold it
and travel the curve
to a center, where some mindless

creature
of the sea
began an architecture.

ii.
I tell my son about
the heavens
and how that cool river
in the sky
is part of a spiral,

how one nebulous arm is
flung out

in space, and that our
large world
is small there, somewhere,
where suns and stars move
like drops
in currents
of water.

I hold an imaginary sphere
in my hand: I am the sun.
And he, the world, runs
around me. Then we stretch
our arms out and turn,
slowly, around and around:
two galaxies on the blue
carpet's

limited
space,

and dizzy and laughing
we fall. We feel the pulse
in the river of veins.
"The universe pulsates,"
I say, "expands, contracts,
and they say it's
saddle-shaped."

  iii.
One night
there will be
horses

and my son will be
one
of the riders
riding
to that cool
river.

The horses will reach
their long
necks

to drink.
The drinking
will fracture
the surface of
stars, sliver
the moon,

circle upon
circle
growing

outward.

I am a rider.
My love is a rider.
My daughters and
my son.

RIVER AND LIGHT

i.

I sit in the marsh
light that is golden
from midnight sun,
from tufts,
cottongrass,
cloudberries.

I sit
hunched
behind a dwarfed
pine,

And I see the female moose
and her calf
walk out
into the light
of the marsh.

She lifts her head.
The long ears listen.
The nostrils read
the inhabitants of the wind.

But the wind comes my way.
Undetected
I remain
locked in my human
smell.

And the female moose
and her calf
bend to drink.

The water is rusty with iron
and rainbow-covered from standing
still between tufts.

The rainbows
stir,
yield to the drinking,
flow in under
velvet nostrils,
to be iron in the hump of the calf,
horn in his crown
and marshlight in the eye of the moose.

I drowse.

A buzzing in my ears
and my eyes open.
I see the head of the cottongrass
letting go,
gathering,
rising,

the spirit of each water hole
deserting its body
to ghost
over the marsh,
Christ on the church wall
ascending.

And I drowse,

until an ax
starts to split morning.
I shiver. Rise.
Walk out of the marsh.

ii.

Once I rode naked on logs
set in their journey
to sawmill
and sea.
I ran out in the water,
caught them in the current,
climbed up and laughed
as they rolled and dunked me
in the river,
to cling, to climb up again
to float, down
stream,
arms out, balancing.

And I swam ashore
when I saw the boys
come down to the river,
to strip their clothes off,
to stand, straight as saplings and
slender, hands
hiding genitals, before
that first plunge
into water.

For I had thought about being
that water.
When my body began to curve
like a river,
I loosened my hair and
floated, head first,
the long hair diffusing around me,
strange undulations,
sea grass,
nipples like pebbles.

Soon as wide in the belly
as the river in spring,
swelling,
covering islands and
willows,
I think about death that is only

water
in lungs, fish and gill
floating down
stream,
the river wide
after thawing.

iii.

Sweet Christ in the morning!
Is there no ultimate
baptismal?

when your belly carries its own
seas,
where some small being
moves through evolutions?

when you wear your mother's dream
of the white bride
and your father's dream
of the bride of Christ?

When you have been patient
in temporary churches,
tents risen to the new
evangelist: "Come.
Come to Christ. Let Jesus wash.
Be purified
in water."

When nothing inside you answered?

I climbed the birch tree,
innocent observer
of bathers and
rowers,
and a white bull was led
and a cow waited,
the cloven-hoofed monster
clumsy on her back,
down,
hit,
hoofs on white hide,
down,
hit,
the long carrot-thing protruding,
up again
and in.

And I climb the stairs
to the abortionist.

iv
But the river –

In early spring
the ice tugs at sandbar
and rock.

Blocks tear
loose,
mad with the weight of
winter
and logs
that someone has axed
or screamed electric saws through,

stripped clean of branches,
brought to the river,
trees
slender as boys
and waiting
for ice-break

Stirs,
and I know
it is not to be
the blood of the lamb
but the blood of a woman
when all her rivers let go
and from her own sea
the child comes, the small face

wise as the three kings
and with all
their giving.
And in some room, golden
with morning
and mooselight
something would have to break free.

Daughter, what do I give you?

1973
Poems
Selected
From:

LETTERS
FROM
THE
ISLAND

For Lena Cronquist and
Göran Tunström

ISLANDERS

The landscape is the same wherever we go;
the snow is melting.
Green hills demand a rocky shore;
more dunes gather.

What can we do? All directions are the same.
The water draws the limit. We know
of differences: the seasons, a catch of fish,
genitals exposed behind the bedroom door.

But we wear the similarities: overalls,
questions to the weather, an unchanging
countenance.

Permanence scares us. We tear the pages,
build a fire, leave the room, turn a corner
in the town.

Down where the road ends, we stand
and talk about delays:
the spring, the storm, the ferry.

LETTERS FROM THE ISLAND

I. *Good Friend,*

My wife gives me a pumpkin
and says: "This is your son."
The pumpkin is large and ripe.
Her belly is flat.

She brings me cabbage,
cucumbers, cauliflower:
"Be careful how you hold
the head."

She will dress them in flannel,
wrap them in blankets,
rock them to sleep.
There is nothing to eat.

At night she walks the island.
Women are in labor. They need
assistance. The carrot is stillborn.
The tomato breaks out of its skin.

We could eat meat. But someone
was bit once, and bled,
and all flesh
became human. We search the rocks

for crabs, set out traps for
lobster, crayfish. But the wind is not
always right. We grow weak.
Our toes tire of clamming.

§

My wife asks: "What were the first

words?" I say:
"In the beginning
God created heaven and earth."

She says: "Stop. That's all I need.
From those come all others."

I hear her talk in the kitchen:
"Fork. Plate." She throws a glass
down. It says its own name. It is
a good name. She throws a cup.

In the garden she rips the pea pods
open, tosses the peas in the air,
naming each one.
The language is changing.

She unravels skein after skein
of blue wool, knits it
in and out of the grass,
praying in tongues.

§

I try to understand.
It is difficult to give birth.
The child might be toad-skinned,
hairy, hoofed.
Its tongue might be cloven. Or worse
the child might be whole
– its own Genesis:
earth divides from heaven,
the land of the child
parts from its mother's
sea.

That Eden is temporary

is understandable, that the child must walk,
with a mate away from his
father,
that he must kill
his brother,
be ready to sacrifice
a son.
Salvation is possible.
The prophets are old.

§

The island is small.
Who do we talk to?
– an old man who says
"Hyacinth isn't a strange name
for a horse. Once I saw
thirty-four horses,
all named Hyacinth."

We gather bark and roots
for dyeing. We store them
in bins. My wife
weaves in the winter.
I write. My father
was a preacher. My son
dances to the bread.

Once my wife painted the walls
in her room: blue daisies,
yellow magpies, red
buttercups.
A tiger unraveled the sun.
A child stepped out of
the sea. It was a good day.
There are many kinds of talking.

II. *Dear Marie,*

I can't write you
today. The people
of the island
are dyeing.

They have saved onion skins
for weeks, peach leaves, grapes,
elderberry.

They have picked marigolds,
St. John's wort, zinnias.
Every plant has a color.
Saffron. Chamomile.

The chokecherry bark in the pot
makes the whole house
smell sweet, as of almonds.

I hear a woman say:
"Beware of lady's bedstraw.
Its roots spread out
like spokes of a wheel.
The roots dye red."

The newlywed one says:
"I fear umbilicaria postulate,
rock-tripe, lichen.
It will dye pink."

The midwife says:
"The red sap of bloodroot
is my only
mandrake."

I hear the voice of my young wife:
"The other day in the meadow,
gathering dyer's thistle,
I was naked. Each pod
I happened to touch
popped open, spilling
its seeds. The dandelion balls
lifted. The milkweed
burst. I had to sit down.
Everything was
so full."

The others laugh, tease
about trolldom and
birthing, whisper:
"You must be pregnant."

My young wife cries: "No!
No!" mixing her dyes:
lady's bedstraw, bloodroot,
umbilicaria postulate.

III *Judith,*

My wife has washed the fleece,
put it in tufts on the bushes
to dry.
The spinning wheel waits:

its rocker is ready, its maiden,
its mother-of-all. The children
call: "Where are our faces?
Where are our fingers and thumbs?
We want to have

voices." I try to approach her.
I start with her fingers,
her thumbs, the whole of her
hands. "My hands understand
every language," she says,

"myself, I am dumb."

111

IV. *Solomon, Dear Solomon,*

I have so much to say.

After my wife delivered,
she went mad.
The child was born whole;
she thought holy.
The fruit of the womb;
any fruit.

Sometimes I think
we have lived too long
in this language.

One day she painted a wall
in the hospital:
Adam and Eve in the garden.
But the doctor painted it over.
White.
One could comprehend:
Eden – outside our sanity.

Why don't you visit?
Thirteen princes
wanted to trade this island
for three shipfuls of spices,
once, so they say.

I don't know.
The flora is rich here.
We make nettle soup
in the spring, dandelion wine
in the summer.
I could use your company.
Though the sign above the door
protects me;
the threshold undermines me.
I question my mother's tongue.
I question my father's language.
I don't understand
deliverance

I have nothing to say.

V. *Daniel,*

It is summer.
A funeral went by my window,
this morning,
thirty-nine old men,
a few old women in black,
one young woman
in cotton.

They walked behind the car,
Abe's station wagon.
I know them all.

When I was small
I dreamt of horses.
I wanted to ride.

In our village
horses were for pulling.

But old man Job
came to the vicarage,
lifted the large orange
bins full of garbage
onto his wagon, and said:
"Come, you can ride."
And winter afternoons
when it was already dark,
we rode to the spring.

There was water at the vicarage,
but this water was sweeter.
Six feet of ice on the river,
but this water was running.

Job dropped the bucket down,
let it fill, hauled it up full,
spilling, gave me a taste,
and filled the barrels
where the stars would rock
as I rode them
home.

It surprised me, I remember,
to think that the writers
of the Bible
knew
our Job. I looked at his face,
to read his suffering.
His wife had died, but already old
he married, again,
a young one.

I don't read the Bible.
But stories come to mind,
and words.
I left the vicarage.
I moved to this island.

I don't have
like Amram, sixteen generations
of rabbis
before me, but there is something
about the word becoming flesh
– and now, flesh becoming
word – that works in us,
slowly,
toward that word's own
holiness.

You understand. You too
are a preacher's son.

IV. *Sally,*

Young women
should wear cotton dresses
with wide skirts.

The wind should come
and fill the dresses,
and the women should rise
like balloons
floating over the land.

I am thirty-three years old.
I celebrated my birthday last month.
My friends brought presents:
photographs of Iceland,
a poem, a shell.
My son gave me a bird.

At thirty-three, Dante knew
his inferno, Jesus was
crucified, St. Augustine
turned from his sins.
I sit on an island.
I write letters.
I count on women
for my visions,
on old men or children,
to be prophets.

The other day the old man said:
"My father lived on a hill.
Three thousand pheasants
were all around the house,
so many, they didn't even mind

if you stepped on their wings."

I count the eggs in the loon's nest
in the spring, mend the broken wing
of the sparrow hawk, think about words,
throw stones in the water.

My wife is in the garden.
Her hands are familiar
with seeds and earth.
There might be another child.
Her fears have
left her.

Today she is wearing a flowered
dress that moves
like an impatient parachute
around her.
A child is laughing
nearby, my son.

VII. *Susanna,*

When I write
I write about places
where I've never been.
And all my letters
are to distant people.

Yesterday I visited
the old man.
They call him mad.
If I don't dream
for a long time,
I feel cheated.

The old man said:
"Who says there are no
flying fish in these
waters? A whole school
of them flew, one day,
right through my sail,
and fell down dead
in the boat. I had to
scoop them up, throw them
out."

§

Sometimes I see people
as horses in a corral,
just standing there,
standing, though any of them
could, at any time, fly
away. When I met my wife,

she lifted her head,
as a young horse would,

sensing something new,
then she looked down
as if to say:
"I have stood here so long.
The possibility of flight
is everywhere. It is the time
of migration. My shoulder blades
ache."

§

We live on an island.
Our feet are large,
holding on to earth.
We walk barefoot,
to feel it better:
gravel, moss,
rock ridges that travel
down to the sea.
We know spring is
dangerous. The beachplum
blooms white. There are
thorns in its branches.
Crucifixions are everywhere.
Ascensions. When our son
was born, I heard
a neighing. I went down
to the barn, whispered
to the horses:

"Fly. Don't fly. Fly."

1975
Poems Selected From:

MOTHER IS

A monster is no more than a combination of parts of real beings.

Jorge Luis Borges

Mare, Mare, Memory
You may not remain with me
Until you count
The birds in the woods
The fish in the river
All the trees
And the words of God

Swedish magic spell read against the Mare, a female creature who was believed to ride sleeping people and animals at night.

Mother's runt and Father's cunt,
Little brown butt,
Fire, my Fire, never go out.
Swedish magic spell read in the evening
when the embers were covered with ashes

MY FATHER'S OLDEST SISTER

never married. Her bed filled
with her body. Her thighs rode
each other. She conceived
a belly. Her arms
cradled her breasts
to sleep.

She was kind, baked for hours:
butter-flaky croissants
and pastries with
marzipan.

When she had eaten, she sat
contented. The chins cuddling close
to each other. Hand holding
hand.

123

MOTHER IS

in an asylum, "obsessed with sexual fantasies."
Fourth of July exploded inside her.
The paper boy threw his genitals on her doorstep.
The milkman brought the cow's very teats
to her box.

"Stop," she moaned, "I can't stand it.
The hotdog man tries to sell me his wares.
The rain is dangerous – all those
umbrellas. I want to be safe
from cucumbers."

I bring her peaches; she scolds: "No. Take them
away. Uptight peaches from a store
cannot come into my mouth
with the sweet juices of orchards.
I want ripe ones I can peel, feel my tongue
follow that ridge. I want to smell of persimmons."

I am a good daughter – the peach tree bloomed again
this spring – but I fear
inheritance. It hurts me to slice the cucumber
and scares me to suck the juice of purple
plums. When the brown iris exposes the hair
that will catch the pollen, I avoid
the garden.

My daughters do the harvesting. I tell them
to be careful. They are laughing
in the kitchen. I read recipes
and sterilize
jars.

MOTHER WAS A GOOD

Catholic.
Each week

she cut the breasts
out of Life.

Every bathing beauty and
sweater girl

was mastectomized
Bikinied bodies

disappeared
above the knee

below the neck:
a window to the following

page (some beer
a car

veterans from
whatever war)

When I married
she said:

My gift is scissors
monogrammed

to cut those things
out of Life.

GRANDMOTHER

baked and cleaned
all day
then washed
herself
in the evening.
Friday

was the best night
of the week.
Grandfather opened the gown
and her breasts
filled his hands
like warm

loaves.
Because the windows
shone, and the sheets
were fresh, her braids
were undone.
When his fingers

opened the folds
of her cunt,
it was like undoing the buttons
and layers of lace
of her high-necked
Sunday
blouse.

DEAD WOMEN

return
to brush
their hair.

They use our combs,
careful not to break
the teeth.

They borrow our brushes,
leaving a trace of hair
in the bristles.

They enter our beds
to feel the warmth of a man
they have almost forgotten,

but not forgotten.
They try on our gloves and soft
scarves.

They try on our nightgowns
and turn slowly
in front of the mirror.

In the morning we wake,
smooth out the gown and scarves
in the drawer, sit in front

of the mirror.
We raise the brush or comb to our heads,
stop, notice the hair,

continue.

MOTHER SAID:

take care of the dolls.
At night they talk
about naked limbs,
blanketless beds,
heads twisted backwards.

Father said:
when you make a fire
in the woods,
don't quench it completely,
leave it for the little people.

I leave the fire in the woods.

128

I listen to the dark.

They say I am not a fish,
because I know how to weave.
They say I am not a woman
because I can live in the water.
Adapted from an entry in a
16th-century chronicle.

TO THE MAN WHO WATCHES SPIDERS

They say we devour our men
after mating.
But you who have watched us
for hours and days,
defend us. Some say

that women who die in childbirth
become spiders that hang in the heavens,
funerary escorts of a dying sun,
while they wait for the day
when they can devour all

of mankind. Tell them,
tell them that we, like women,
know perfection, that we lose it
quickly, that we hide the loss
in a growing, terrifying

art. Aging
we sit and spin, uncertain
that someone could love us,
seeing us.

LETTER FROM PETER WILKINS

*According to an ancient chronicle, Peter Wilkins was shipwrecked
and came to an Antarctic island, where a race of winged creatures lived. He tried to teach them Christianity and wrote a
history about his experiences... then he left for England.*

I was not dead when you left me.

You thought me beautiful
and loved me.
You admired my arms' ability
to become
wings. You rushed

your fingers through my white
feathers, found my nipples
in the down, touched me
until I knew another
flying.

But it was too easy
to pull my quills
when you needed a pen
– to write your
history.

I tried to believe in a god
who flew only once,
but as I see my sisters rise
over the Antarctic,
I question. I question.

THE DWARFS

Our faces are like other faces.
Perhaps that is the worst.
It is the lack of proportion
that matters.

Our arms are stunted –
as if they never reached for someone.
Our legs are too short –
as if the road was not long enough.

There are no clothes
ready to be worn by us,
no chairs built for us,
no bed that we can fill.

131

Like children we want someone to lift
us, to hold us high above the crowds,
to see the parade, the circus,
the display window.

We avoid mirrors, but it grows dark,
and car windows and fenders become
reflectors. We move through them
reminded: it is the lack of

proportion that matters. So we live
together. Our hands
are the same size. Our eyes see
on the same level.

TWINS

We wear the same clothes:
dresses, coats and hats
fill our closet
like animals the ark.
Shoes and gloves come
by fours.

Our hair is parted on the same
side. We have rings on the same
finger. We play
the piano. We bite
our nails. Our beds
are close together.

But her ribbons choke me
in my sleep. I awake
and her smile in my mirror
fractures
my features.

When she eats my food, tears
my dress and destroys the bird's
nest, I am God's angel.
When she is good, I beat her
in my dreams and pray:
Let her be evil.

PANE DOLCE

The women of unleavened dough
have many breasts.
The young men of Frescati
hesitate, then laugh,
as each one tears a breast off
and eats it.

Mayaul has 400. I have two.
Mathematics leaves no room
for interpretation.
Neither milk nor honey flows,
but I hold them up to you.
It is a human
offering.

MISS PIMBERTON OF

the Metropolitan
Museum of
Art
has the key
to
Genitalia.
The broken off

parts
of
Greek statues and
Roman gods
are her
curatorship.
From foreign countries

and graves,
Papal quarters and
geological digs,
they find their way
to
Miss Pimberton,
who dates

the testicles, measures
penises,
labels all –
and files them
neatly,
deliberately,
working late.

MY RIGHT EYE

is a hawk
that circles all night
looking for the small mice
of dreams
to run out from under
my pillow.

My left eye is an owl
alert in its hollow
waiting for nightmares to come
on the wings of bats.
In the morning

I am the predator
returning from my hunt,
the gatherer come back
to my nest.
My family is fed.
My eyes ache.

THE BEASTS HAVE ENTERED

the cloister my human face
says I am manticore my love
my wound: unicorn Christ
I have looked for the bird
and the snake and the song
plumage of heaven poisonous
sting and found it chiseled
in marble and stone then who
speaks in my dream of the
two-headed monster: one head
awake while the other sleeps

What shall I do? My man compares
me to a wild flower.
When I have withered in his hands,
he will leave me.
Aztec poem

PEACHES

There was a contest
once
for the best picture
of a peach

in China

Madame Ling
or was it Ching
sat in some yellow
pollen

then

carefully, again
she sat
upon
a piece of white

paper

137

SHE USED TO WATER THE PLANTS

twice a week
then
every morning
then she started to transplant
take cuttings
fertilize

she moved the plants outdoors
in the spring: more room
more light
she planted seeds, grafted trees
sprayed roses and pruned

she said the common names
of the flowers, softly
as if they were children
then the Latin
forming the words with care
a stilted music, lovely and

foreign "a flower bed
is as good a bed as any"
she said
when her husband left her
there was not question
of loss

he returned once
carried her in from the garden
washed the soil off her feet
and cleaned the dirt from under her nails
with a paring knife

in the morning
the bed was full of crushed leaves
and small clouds of yellow
pollen

LEMONS, LIMES

The moon, aye,
I suck on green fruit.
It is appropriate.
Lemon moons in the trees
and their small green sisters.

I pucker my mouth
and speak to Theresia.
I don't know who she is.
I like the sound of the word
"terrestrial."

There is a thicket in my head
and bells that can break
an eardrum
– as the sun, the retina,
the moon, the membrane of the sea.

No one drowns in the ocean.
It is just a matter of listening
to someone else's heart,
letting something else take over
the breathing.

NIGHTSHADE

We turn off the bedroom light
and the windows grow branches.
The darkness grows leaves.
Herbs cover the carpets.

And the women come.
They look for rosemary, chaste tree,
betony, to give them good dreams.

They look for sweetbay and roses,
mint and madonna lily.
They want fair skin.

A young wife looks for primrose
and wallflower. She wants to be
fruitful.

A nursing mother looks for fennel
to keep her breasts
full. My husband and I

do not mind them:
we have slept in the growing
nightshade so long.
We move close to each other.

The flowers that we are
open. Petals, pollen.
We lick each other clean.

SPELL

Blessed Rose, Peony,
Deliver me from evil
Make the child's journey
Smooth.

Like to the She-wolf
The cubs have clawed
The inside of my
Belly.

Peony seed will heal me.
Love will tear me.
Thunder will deliver me.
Blessed Rose.

THE
JUGGLER

I drink my coffee
black
like the iris of
my sister's
eyes
showing
a smaller me
little sister
in the white
cup

AT NIGHTFALL

The women leave the funeral procession. They untie their scarves and spread them on the grasses. They unbutton their skirts and hang them on the branches. They roll down their stockings and let them float down the river. Darkness slips out of the sleeves of their blouses. Long black hair colors the wind.

If the dead man drowned, scales of fish will glitter above them. If the dead man burned, flames of the fire will cover the heavens. If the dead man was shot, a silver moon will grow from the bullet. If he died far away, black horses will ride him home.

145

IF HE HAD NOT HAD TWO HANDS
TATTOOED ON HIS CHEST
for Sally

If Michelangelo had not painted God reaching his hand
toward Adam If Adam had not reached his hand toward
God If I had not wanted to be alone by the lake If the
young man had not asked me to teach him how to swim
If he had not had two hands tattooed on his chest If I had
given him more warning about the depth of the water If I
had not swum out to a rock in the lake If I had not turned
to see him following me If he had not had two hands
tattooed on his chest If I had not started to swim back
toward him If I had not told him not to struggle If I had
not reached out my hand If the tips of his fingers had not
brushed mine As he slipped down in the water Without a
word Without a cry To be found three hours later tangled
in sea weed I would not have walked away calm Not grieving Then grieving As if God had not touched Adam.

OFFERING

For years we shared the same pillow, and nothing knew my body like his hand. So when it began, that very familiarity became part of the disguise. The fact that he knew my skin to be soft hid the fact of feathers that, in some aviary puberty, started in softest down. Because he had always teased about the sharpness of my elbows and shoulder blades, it seemed natural to hide their changing from his touch. Was it foresight or accident that he had called me egret woman and said that sparrows sleep their morning in my hair? At midnight, after the kiss was done, and he had loved in the hollow of my nest, my lips shrank, curving their shells into a beak. My eyes grew small and round. The light from moon and cloud or snow, that gently touched the darkness of the room, began to burn and beg me to come out. The walls that used to hold us warm against the wind began to shake their lock and chain. It had been right for him to sprawl, dreaming in that feathered bed, a leg casually forgotten on my leg, but now I withdrew my foot to hide its claw and buried my face to quench the cackle and the caw. I left the room each night not wanting him to see me such, or scare at the awareness of my touch. I flew, shying away from branches and eaves, hunting the creatures of the night. At dawn he questioned the heap of mice outside the door and the dead owl upon the stair. I told him that I loved him, as I brushed my hair. Loving, a being gives whatever offering he can.

THE SERVANTS OF THE EMPEROR

Since someone did urge me to go,
as a son, can I delay for a moment?
It is true that you have been cast
adrift on the sea because of me, but
circumstances are also responsible.
Cho'e Pu

It is true that you have been cast adrift because of me,
but circumstances are also responsible. The wish of the
Emperor is stitched in his robe and talks in its sleep, when
the storms gather. You have all heard the voices. I only
united you and supervised the choice of ship and rigging.
One could have said that on that morning each of you
wore the sun's very face, for eagerness shone about you.
Now you walk the deck with faces as pale as the moon,
for the moon has touched you, and you do not know which
one of you will be the next to slip overboard, to rock
forever on the swell that lifts its tide toward you. Fish
has always been good food, and seaweed spread on rice,
still filling the barrels, but now you think food from the
sea is death itself feeding you, so you slice the raw fish
into small pieces, eat as little as possible and toss the rest
to the birds that follow us. You are growing younger and
younger each day of the journey, and I see you stand in
the aft looking out, spelling the garden path, the pogo
stick, the little friend pouring tea at the imaginary cer-
emony. Anything that has ever been grows words, detailed
with the stones and flowers of the land, and each human
act remembered is linked to the foot that taps the floor
of forest or house, river bridge or mountain path, like a
heart beat. I know you are becoming children, though
you hide under your blankets at night, your hands covering the place of your manhood. The warmth of your hand
wakes it to swell, but its swelling, its moon liquid re-

minds you that the moon itself is your only concubine.
You pray for wind. You pray that the celestial dragon will
devour the pearl of the moon. You pray that storm clouds
will come to continue creation. But the dragon is sleeping on the Emperor's robe, and the sea remains a mirror
where the moon can watch you, even when you sail into
your dreams. I would ring the temple bell, offer the whit-
est rooster, give my youngest daughter and the quince of
every season, to sail you into a harbor where you can touch
earth and woman again, but only moonlight flies the rigging, and the phoenix that rises each morning burns you
as you scrub the deck. Which one of us will be the next
to quench the call for mother in the water? The journey
toward death is clean and pure, for the servants of the
Emperor.

149

THE ANGEL OF DEATH

Because she wanted me, I slipped out of my skin. I thought it would fall like unnecessary clothing in the corner, by the chair, but it was my skin that went to her, like a beige trench coat flying through the air.

Somewhere near the flue of the fireplace or beside the open window, she waited, calling me, and the hairs of my arms lifted their small antennae and listened. Tired of holding the body in place all these years, the skin broke loose, my empty hands flapping like gloves. Death must be something to hold on to.

In my nakedness, I stood there, white like a sprout is white before it reaches the air. Small white breasts, short white hair, white fringes of lashes around my colorless eyes. And skinless I could perceive all the small angels in things: dancing on the head of a pin, in the leg of a table, in the arm of the chair. Even in the air there were tiny galaxies spinning, as if it were Midsummer, and the dance had started. Then something stirred at the base of my spine. A warm coating started to spread, licking its long tongue over my surfaces, the elbow, the hip, the raspberry of my nipple, until each pore, mole, curve and mark was covered. Colors came back. The earlobes hung like drops from my ears, asleep, not listening.

But the angel of death is somewhere, watering my flowers, reading over my shoulder, counting the days of the moon. She tells me that invisible things exist: angels, molecules, the green horses of the grass.

EVENT

i.

Look at a yellow flowering tree.
Think about a red
bird.

ii.

Think about a white flowering tree
and· a blue
bird.

iii.

Write an anti-war poem. Use a tree
and a bird. For example:
no tree, no
bird.

iv.

Look for the branches. Make a flute
out of the bird's hollow
bones.

v.

Play.

THE SHIPBUILDER

I can't divulge the secret of the narrow neck,
or tell if the mast must bend,
or explain ropes secured or lines attached.
The flag that flies in the invisible breeze
and the anchor that holds on
must remain a riddle to those
observing schooners in transparent domes.

(on a mantelpiece, a fireplace)

When I was ten, I spelled a note
of imagined desperation: "Rescue me!"
rolled it up, put it in a bottle, sent it out to sea,
and I wrote, beside a river: "Rescue is coming,"
and let the river rock its promise
down stream. Now I build
ships in bottles.

(for mantelpiece, fireplace)

Have you seen
the skin on the face of old women
grow transparent, as if their very bones
are straining at their rigging, ready
for their sails to unfurl,
to float away

forever?

     (Rescue, rescue me)

I can't divulge the secret of the narrow neck,
or tell if the mast must bend,
or explain ropes secured or lines attached.
As I fit the unfittable plank and nail,
paint the name of the ship, detail, detail
to be miraculously there,
locked inside glass,

     (for mantelpiece, fireplace)

I pray I will not construct my mother's face.

A CHILD CALLED MORTE

Now is the time,
the children grown,
that we must let
the new child in,
wake for its crying
need at night,
hold it close
when it is scared
and scares us.
Having been parents
for so long,
we can disobey
the rules,
let the child sleep
in our bed,
tease it, feed it,
at the touch of whim.
Perhaps we shouldn't
use its name
as one hesitates to say
the name of someone
who is gone
or too much desired.
Nuzzling close below my chin,
or resting in your open palm,
it waits, smaller than a nest
or bird itself,
or speckled egg,
unbreakable.

THE VISITOR

If you open the door some evening
and there is nobody there,
don't be alarmed.
You heard the bell
and steps on the stairs.
Let the emptiness enter.

Make room on the couch.
Hang her coat on the chair.
Move the roses away from her face.
There is a reason she has come
and she will tell you.
There is a reason you opened the door.

And if you find
the stillness of the room has skin,
if evening lets its long hair down,
if the bed pulls you
and the body of the dark covers you,
who is to say what is real or not real,

if you fall asleep on your back,
your hands open to the shape of breasts.

THE JUGGLER

I had practiced for years. Whenever I had a chance, I juggled with oranges, plates, pine cones, pennies. My uncle encouraged me, though my mother said: The boy should do something better. He should read. He should learn to make a living. She said: If your father were alive, he would show you. But I didn't stop. How could I stop? There was always some space above my hands calling me. Behind a tree, behind a tent, behind a truck, on the other side of field, there was always this space where I could be God throwing the planets, or the wind commanding the leaves.

On the night of the first kiss, the air touched my hands in some new way. I juggled soft skin, Lena's lips, not quite open, her lapel, my own chin, the two pimples by my ear. My hands were clumsy. I almost dropped something, but caught it just in time. I juggled No, Well, Maybe, Yes. The director saw me. The boy is not so bad, he said. Give him some time in the third ring. I juggled lights. I juggled time. I juggled sound.

On the night I first entered a woman, the lights danced out of my hands. I juggled hair and lips and breasts and vulvae. I juggled small wet spaces that could suck me into some sweet oblivion I mastered. I juggled a soft curtain, a blood stain, my own organ swelling. The music lifted me. I juggled applause and more applause. I juggled a soft voice calling me.

On the night my son was born, there was nothing to throw. My hands were empty, waiting. There was a strange fear inside me. The music was building, the lights were on me, but nothing happened. Until out of all that waiting, something came. I could reach my hand up into that waiting space, and suddenly there was a small shape, settling to the shape of my hand. My hand fell, rose, lifted high, fell again, and all things in the world were attached to my hand, rising, falling, holding, protecting.

On the night the girl died, my hands were independent objects moving without me. A broken leg, a cut thigh, some blood-stained clothing, a sequined ribbon, all tore out of me, pulling at the skin, exposing the bone, catapulting with a small scream out of my hands, to fall back to the space of my palms with a moan. The lights were on me, but I didn't juggle them, they juggled me. In the dark space of the tent, I bounced up and down, while the music of my own voice came from some strange distance, a slow heartbeat of sound repeating. No. No. No. No.   157

LETTER FROM THE SNAKE WOMAN

Señor, I am glad you recognize me. Rattling is a poor substitute for speech. They say my tongue is forked and fear me, but it is an attempt to speak an honest language between man and God that divides me. The earth never leaves me. I move across it with the motion of waters, at home in such dry places as desert, prairie, mountains of rock. My spirit becomes bird and flies out of my flesh. It hurts to change skin. I lock my head to my tail and hold the world in the loop. I circle your finger. Eve listened to me. The Greeks saw me wise and named me. The Indians know me. I am the song in encantadora. Call me Sofia. I have been here before.

158

1978
Poems
Selected
From:

COLOR
POEMS

There are six chairs
to be painted
blue.
I have no time
for poems.
But
six chairs painted
blue
could be considered,
most concretely,
six blue
poems.

WHEN IT IS SNOWING

the bluejay
is
the only piece of sky
in my
back yard.

YELLOW BLOUSE

We meet
by the water
fall

I am wearing
my yellow
blouse

It is almost
daffodils
spring

I would be
a thousand
springs
under you

If you
unbutton
my blouse

THE RED GLOVES

I am returning
the red
gloves
you left in Vera's
pocket

They are soft shells
that miss
the snails that would give them
their own slow
speed

They are five-room houses
waiting for their inhabitants
to come home

They are red wings
that have forgotten
how to fly

When you receive them
put them on

for like puppies who warm each other
all night
you will warm them
and they will warm
your hands

which must be
lost
Valentines
without their red
envelopes

WHITE SANDALS

I put on my white
sandals
and go
to the city

My feet are large
but my sandals know
the delicacy of
birdcages, gazebos,
garden rooms with
white wicker
chairs

164   When I enter
your room,
you unbuckle
the tiny buckles,
undo the slender
white straps
and let my feet
out

so that they can
run through the air
when we love

while on the floor
the white cages of
my sandals discuss
the definition
of birds

THE BLACK BIRD
for Keith Abbott

While we talked
a bird flapped its large wings
above your left shoulder.
When I took my eyes away from yours
and looked at the bird,
it changed into a shadow of leaves
that moved outside the window.
Back inside your eyes I knew
the bird was still there.
Caged in no cage
it would remain,
flapping its large wings
incessantly
and without
a sound.

165

POLEMICS

There are things we must not do:
pick a flower and throw it away,
dismiss the spirit of a tree,
flood a field that does not need water,
ignore a child,
turn away from the voice of love.

There are holy places
for moose, for Lapps, for death.
We must know them in our bones.
Pappa, do you see the two-headed reindeer calf
running in the magenta
fireweed?

166

MINNESOTA EVENT

Leave the green bottle where the water touches the shore. The ship that broke in three will find its way, growing smaller and smaller in death. It will slip in through the narrow neck, mending in the cold. Unaware of their size, the sailors will return to their posts, reading charts, battling storms, wondering why the lakes in this world are domed by such a green sky.

THE BLUE HORSE

I have accepted the fact that he follows me. I used to be self-conscious, turn away, look in different directions, but it is difficult to hide a blue horse on a plane, in a store, at a cocktail party. I have learned that if I give him a piece of sugar, he won't eat the gladiolas. If I stroke his mane gently, he will walk carefully on the carpets. Children like the blue horse and come to play. He is gentle. Their parents are scared, or awkward, and ask what you feed a blue horse, or if he is naked. Now I answer each invitation: I can come if I can come with the blue horse. And if I go, and if I speak about him, a meadow that's greener than green grows around him, becomes a green cloud slowly rising. If we reach up, pick a violet or a bachelor's button, the place where the flower was becomes a small hole through which we can see the blue horse. When I go to sleep in the evening, he brings me blankets of Oriental poppies and timothy, dandelion leaves and rose petals. Then he stands there all night, eating slowly, while I sleep.

THE WILD GEESE

Confused, last spring, the geese flew north and south
and north again, to nest, I thought,
until their honking pulled my thoughts along,
as they were flying south.
I don't know how many times
they traversed my window's checkered space,
but each time I thought, yes, it's spring.
Then the questions settled in.

It is summer now. I think I should put my pink
blouse on and go into the city. Or strip
my clothes off, swim. Or look for red
among tomatoes that insist on being green.
But instead, I sit in an unmade bed
with paper, pen. Instead of going out,
I travel in, and out again, and in. The wild geese

are looking for a place. Close your face.
Close the lakes of your eyes, or I might settle in.

SHEETS

*Methinks that white-lead chapter about whiteness is but a
white flag hung out from a craven soul.*
                              Herman Melville

Leaving you, I say: "It's with a heavy heart." Then I laugh,
thinking of the sad old president. But the laugh comes
out of my mouth as if I were carrying someone else's face,
for in the place where the heart should be, the woman
who takes in washing is beating, wringing, mangling
sheets. There is always a reason: that they have flown like
a white albatross into a strange country, that they must
be ready to fly again, or spread on a bed, smooth, white,
smelling of wind. It's a practical world, and I understand
house-keeping. But it's with a heavy heart.

PROVERBS

i.

Early to bed
I miss his loving.
Early to wake
I miss my dream.

In the evening I sleep
on the shoulder of my pillow.
In the morning I eat
the worm.

ii.

I go from tree to tree
questioning what
my daughter does.
I mark the spot
where each apple fell
and calculate
the distance.

iii.

I would go as far
as the crow flies
to come to the place
where one can erase
the sins of the father,
but each morning I wake
to the warning of red
skies; each night I forget
in the delight
of sailors.

iv.

There is such a distance between
the birds in the bush
and my hands.

WHITE

Silence
has so many
voices.

1984
Poems
Selected
From :

LETTERS
FROM
THE
FLOATING
WORLD

Ukiyo-E is a Japanese genre of wood-block printing, presenting scenes of everyday life.

E means "picture," "painting," or "image." Ukiyo can be translated "the floating world," "the fleeting world," "the world of the senses," "the world of sorrow," or "the ordinary world."

UKIYO-E

What explanation is given for the phosphorus light
That you, as boy, went out to catch
When summer dusk turned to night?
You caught the fireflies, put them in a jar,
Careful to let in some air,
Then you fed them dandelions, unsure
Of what such small and fleeting things
Need, and when
Their light grew dim, you
 Let them go.

There is no explanation for the fire
That burns in our bodies
Or the desire that grows, again and again,
So that we must move toward each other
In the dark.
We have no wings.
We are ordinary people, doing ordinary things.
The story can be told on rice paper.
There is a lantern, a mountain, whatever
 We can remember.

175

Hiroshige's landscape is so soft.
What child, woman, would not want to go out
Into that dark, and be caught,
And caught again, by you?
I want these pictures of the floating world
To go on, but when
The light begins to dim, catch me.
Give me whatever a child imagines
To keep me aglow, then
 Let me go.

ON THE OTHER SIDE OF UJI BRIDGE

I sit on a stone by a pond
Watching a turtle swim.
A tiny turtle swims
In the shadow of the larger one.
Earlier, on the steps of the outer
Shrine, I heard a whistling,
Whistling, and looked up to see
A white hawk circling,
Circling, to then disappear
With the clear note
Of his calling.

Is this what I came to find,
Traveling alone, the only
Caucasian on the train, at each
Station inquiring: "Ise?"
While trying to read signs
I could not understand.

It is autumn. The river
Is almost dry. The bridge across,
Like the inner and outer shrine,
Is rebuilt every twenty years,
According to instructions given
A thousand years ago.

I did not know
Why I had to come here, to finger
The wooden fence of the enclosure,
To sit on a stone. My children
Are grown. The twenty-year
Cycle of the marriage is done.
A singular note circles toward
Heaven. Let the instructions
For disassembling and reassembling
Of inner and outer shrine
Be in a language

I can understand. For it is
The month without gods,
And in the Emperor's forest,
Where cryptomeria and cypress
Have grown for a thousand years,
The hardwoods are burning.

IN THE LAND OF SHINAR

In the land of Shinar
The buildings grow more and more
Complex. The expert in art and
Mass communications says:
A civilization can be measured
By the permanence of its buildings.
On the receiving end of
The television signal, I want to argue:
What about Ise? Is its permanence
In the idea or the construction?

It grows more and more difficult
To communicate. Our adult language
Is rich in words we can speak
And spell, but understanding is
Illusive. The three letters of the
Marriage vow are easy to pronounce,
But the promise is challenged, when
The body proves impermanent.
Until death do us part is dismissed
As an embarrassing remnant

From some previous age, like God.
The reason for reaching toward
Heaven is forgotten, yet the walls
Grow tall. Although we can see
Each other through the glass,
Our words are muffled. We have to
Change the I said and You said
To Once upon a time, in the land
Of Shinar. Maybe Ciardi was
Not such a fool, when
He pronounced you cannot

Become a poet in a language
That is not your mother tongue.
Perhaps he meant that we need
To use the simple language
We spoke as children, the one we
Use, or do not need to use, when
We lie next to each other,
Spelling the word home – and
Admitting that a discourse like

This is not necessarily a poem.
It is just the babble of someone who
Does not want to get lost in Babel,
When the only certainty regarding
The future of the flesh is its lack
Of future, someone who thinks that
The only burning of books should be
In the Alexandrian fire of the spirit,
Where human histories can be housed,
Reaching, or not reaching, to heaven.

OVID

for David Ignatow

Who has not been exiled
From some civilization,
And forced to live
With the Barbarians
To then be resigned
That civilization
Is only a construction
In the mind
And language
Simply a convenient tool
Used when planning the hunt
Or commenting on the direction
Of the wind?

And yet,
When the years have passed
And your hearing is impaired,
And your eyes almost blind,
You, the trusted prisoner,
Walk out of the encampment,
To go, simply to go
Toward that place in the mind,
Knowing that no cities will rise
Out of the sea of rushes,
And no poets will expound
On the meaning of a line
Or explain the ways of the gods.

And as an old man
Finally sees he has been
The brunt of a joke,
You stop, scratch your head,

And laugh. To wind and marsh
You declare: "When I was exiled
From civilization, I thought I was
Exiled from civilization!"

And then,
When you finally begin to understand
How the Barbarian body
Accepts the civilization in the mind,
You trip
Over a tuft, or slip
In the brackish water of a puddle.
You can't get up. But
It's all right.

You have let your aging body expand
Because you wanted to include
Everything. Now it refuses
To heed your command.
But if there is a joke,
It is on the gods, or time.
For you have your talisman
From the wilderness
And the old dreams,
Recognized as dreams.

The world without has already lost
Its clear sounds and sharp delineations,
So your visions are intact
And will remain
When the heron
Lays an egg in the ear
That held your hearing
And the eye of a blackbird will spy
A gray hair she can twist
Into a nest.

THE ACROBAT

There is no bravery in flight.
    There are only laws
        Of four-dimensional geometry
And a body tracing spiral and arc
    Of a predetermined trajectory
        That sends me off with ease
Leaving the platform to leap
    From trapeze to trapeze.

It is not the gravity of earth
    Pulling all things closer
        That scares me,
But the gravity of love that attracts
    And urges me to let go,
        To trust that you will catch me,
The way practice has taught me to trust
    The sky, my brother, and combined mastery.

So if I dared to stand
    Barefoot on the ground before you,
        My face close to your face,
Hand to hand, a fear of heights
    Would somersault inside me
        At the thought of leaping out
Into the space your eyes offer
    To hold me.

SHUNGA

The night opens the pillow book
and shows us
ourselves.

In stages of dress and undress
our genitals seem to grow
out of proportion.

Flute of jade, moon-flower.
The lucky numbers
are odd.

Three irises in the blue and white
bowl, in spring, chrysanthemum,
in autumn.

Hidden by the fan of darkness,
my shoulder is almost bare.
You touch it.

On the bell-shaped lid of
the Chinese jar, a child
is playing.

NIGHT AND DAY

"Look at the pigeons," you say
And we watch a flock
Fly out over the street, to loop
Back toward the roofs, showing first
The soft gray of their bellies,
Then their darker side.

In Escher's woodcut,
The light birds fly toward a dark
Town, while the spaces between them
Are dark birds flying toward a light
Town. I have lived with Night and
Day for years. Now that I am aware

Of my aging, only such opposites
Make sense. Like Ann, I will stand
In a dark pool, observing how my light
Skin, and the muscles beneath,
Are changing. Everyone is aging.
And yet, when I stand here looking up,

I am aware of the dark space
Under the light skin of my belly,
Our child, and the light that would
Fly, in the dark of his eyes,
As he lifts his face toward the sky,
Because you say, "Look at the pigeons."

APRIL FOOL

There are too many poems where
A lesser Hamlet confronts himself
In the poor Yorick of some historic
Place. Lines seldom measure up
To emotions evoked by such traveling.
Hence I have vowed to abstain.
      But
When some jubilant bird taunts me
With the intricacies of his song
To memorize the cadence and recall
Its name, I think of the iris blooming
In the Forum –
      And how we would go,
With bread and cheese and wine,
To compare the hues of blue
And argue about the names: Iris
Florentina, Palladia, Variegata,
Spuria – What is Romulea Columnae?
      And then
Pay close attention to the choice of place,
Where we would sit in the sun,
The old walls
      Just something to lean on.

FATA MORGANA

This is the Strait of Messina.
The images rise. They are real.
Castles in the air are inhabited.
The reflected evening light spills
Over windowsills. At dusk
Someone touches a light switch here
Or there, and vertical checkerboards,
With squares randomly lit, rise
In the night. What fool would dare
To explain the rules, or determine
Who is queen and who is knight?

This very tree, this very field,
The very woods beyond, all so richly
Green, on a summer day, are soft gray
In the morning. How could this be
So, if we believe in what we know?
Green is green. If we believe in
What we see, this very tree, this
Very field, the very woods beyond
Pull loose and rise, to float
Above the ground. What is the sound
Of an explanation? The line of vision

Bends. Distant lands appear or

Disappear. Who is the one viewing
The island we are floating on? Tell me,
Are we still below the horizon?
The color of your eyes is constant.
The answer to the question about hands
Is touch. Stay near. There is much
I do not understand. Though I do not
Fear the changes, I must know them
In your hair, your skin. The tide is
Coming in. Let's go down to see

The sun lose its roundness, grow
Squat and set, its reddest lip upon
The horizon – or observe the familiar
Disk breaking apart, one section rising;
The other slipping into the ocean,
A common illusion this time of evening,
While we discuss some version of this
Life and the baseless fabric of our vision.

III UKIYO-E
IMAGES FROM THIS WORLD OF SORROW

ICE FISHING
for Olof Lagercrantz

When the world is frozen
And the surface of the water
Lets all men walk
As if they were sons of God,

You walk across the white of the lake
To the hole you have chopped in the ice,
Push the ax handle against the iris
That has formed since yesterday,
Ease the weighted line down
Into the dark pupil
And wait.

It is winter,
But below you the fish are swimming
Slowly, as a summer
Memory, or a dream of spring,

And you think about the perch that will sizzle
In the frying pan, the meat prices in the village,
The war that was and the one that threatens,
And like the fish below,
You move now and then,
So that your hands and feet
Won't grow numb

In the cold.
And just as you wonder
If the mythic pike, like God,
Really exists,
The one who has torn your nets

Through the years, avoided your trolling,
Tangled your lines
In the rushes,

Your line starts to slip
Away, and you know it is he.
You wrestle. But all your skill
And human strength is for naught.
The pike pulls. The white edge
Around the dark hole gives way.
God's eye opens, and you disappear.

But the fish stories continue
To tell about the great pike
That exists, or does not
Exist, that is caught,

Or never caught,
The one who pulls the fisherman onward,
Across the waters,
Promising to answer
The prayer of the hungry, the one who calls
In your sleep, when the current
Is strongest, or on the day

When the world is frozen
And the surface of the water
Lets all men walk
As if they were sons of God.

189

THE NAIL OF THE INDEX FINGER
for Robert Lowell September 14, 1977

In a Washington of poetry readings
And peace demonstrations,
We cruised the lit monuments.
"Jefferson," you said and filled
The space of the dark with a joke.
"Lincoln," you said and quoted
The Greeks. In a small bar
You pulled the bound galleys of *Notebooks*

Out of your pocket.
"Do you like this change?" you asked.
"Do you understand?"

190

When we said good night,
You took my hand and observed it
For a long time, as if it were a visitor
From a strange country.
And still holding mine
You pointed to the nail
of your own index finger.
"This too will die," you said,
"Imagine, this too will die."

In the sunshine of the next day,
We walked up Capitol Hill
To lunch with your old friend, my new friend.
You gave him the bound galleys.
The three of us laughed.
But during the meal I grew silent
Feeling, for the first time in years,
Like a little girl in the company of grown-ups
Who never will die.

Today I know
Words are only
One hand clapping;
The flesh is the other hand.

THE CLOWN

This is my real face.
White is right for skin
And red for bulbous nose.
My mouth an enormous grin.
The vertical black lines
That slit my eyes assure
The split vision of a clown.
I tumble, fall. Balance
Is a word not understood
At all, and grace, a quality
Made up like my face.

Have you seen me on the wire?
I walk and stumble, stumble,
Slip. Slip and start to fall.
Catch my fall and slip again.
You laugh in recognition, for
I am your vision of yourself.
The baggy pants – the world
You cannot fill. The tiny
Coat – the dream you outgrew
Long ago, but wear. The bow
Tie – your attempt to brightly
Face the world, and rightly.
My broken shoes – your open
Mouth. The patch of hairless
Scalp and round beflowered

Hat – the crown
To the kingdom of absurdity.

And if
I peel off paint and putty,
What is the nose whose back
Is narrow as a sparrow's beak?
What is the empty mouth?
What is the vision in each tiny
Eye? What is the hairless
Scalp below the hat? My walk
Is your walk. I tumble, lose
My pants, stumble, fall and
Cry. And you can laugh at that.

193

A RACCOON

A raccoon lies broken
On the broken lines of a road.
Like the car that killed it,

I speed by. I have seen the pain
In the small and pointed face
And blinked at the pink entrails

That trail from its belly.
But it is the paw that makes me
Stare. What is there that makes the paw

Reach up? and the five fingers
At the end of the reach, bend
Like a hand? They say

That animals are our innocence,
What we were before Eden
And the Fall. Though I cannot

Understand it all, I stay on my side
Of the broken line that divides
The going from the coming.

ONNA-E, PICTURES OF WOMEN

I. *A Sentence*

In a Victorian mansion
Filled with Persian carpets,
Billiard tables inlaid with ivory,
Stained glass windows and mahogany
Balusters,
There is a white-haired woman,
Who ignores the inherited surroundings
Preferring to be in the cellar,
Where, with electric tools, she discovers
The faces in the stones she finds
On the shore of Lake Superior.

II. *Exposing Fox and Artifice*

Atlas cedar from Africa and
Cut-leaf maple from Japan
Presented, respectively,
The most foreign cones and
Colors. Something to observe,
She said. And admire. But
Manicured lawns were not
Her habitat. The forest
More than romanticism.
She missed the woods
He took away from her, faltered,
Made extensive journeys
In her mind,
Collected words, lost her sense
Of direction.
From Montana, and a stranger,
Came a warning:
When you lose your instincts,
You die.
Contrarily, she stayed alive,
But exorcised his picture
From her album.
When she heard the story of
The Spartan youth who let a fox
Gnaw at his flesh, rather
Than having a lie
Exposed,
She tore her green shirt open.

III. *Susanna*

Mirrors are passive observers,
Watching her dry herself slowly.
But the reflection in the lake
Scares her. Trees and rocks
Move closer. Sky and water
Touch her. As she sees the soft
Shapes of her body break apart
In the ripples, to fuse again,
In stillness, she knows she can
Die and live forever. The story
About the Elders is metaphor.
It is time that ravishes. Because
She has heard about the old woman
Who wondered what haggard spirit
Was hiding in the water where
Her young face should be reflected,
Susanna dances.

IV. *The Story of Toile*

Far from the French countryside,
Peasantry or aristocracy,
She covered the dining room walls
Of her split-level house
With a blue-printed toile
And filled the rococo cupboard
With blue and white china,
Decorated with scenes
Of an imagined Orient.

"The universe is complete,"
She said, "The cosmos grows
In my backyard."

Then the magician came.
With his tricks he fast-talked
Love, flipped the cards and
Her mind. Name the four beasts
Of the Apocalypse.
When he left, she dropped a cup.
She could not understand
That all magic might be
Sleight of hand.

V. *Blanc de Blanc*

Late-winter afternoons
She sits in the white room
Drinking black coffee,
While the windows lay
Their checkerboards of light
On the white carpet
And elongated plaids of light
Slip around the white
Couches.

She could sip Campari
Or some more exotic apéritif
And insist she dreams in color.
Instead she observes
The approaching equinox
That will divide the light
And lack of light
Of day and night
Equally.

Outside the pane
Oblivious of cliché,
The sunset burns

By the gazebo.
In a few days it will rest
In the crown of the pear tree,
Then the apple tree,
To silhouette the hemlock,
Come summer.

Whalebone is out of date,
Brocade reserved for the ambassador's
Reception. Mondrian has influenced
The decor. Decorum is
A question. So what shall she do
When the house is in mourning,
When body and soul want to
Fly away home, when the children
Are leaving?

FIVE STANZAS FOR MY TWO BROTHERS

*A red rose reflects only red light
because it absorbs all the other colors
of the spectrum.*
                              Isaac Newton

i.

The roses of my brother's eyes
Absorb all colors but blue,
Pale blue roses blooming,
Absorbing the green roses of the grass,
Absorbing the wet roses of rivers,
Closing their sky petals around
The black roses of pupils
Seeing roseacia's
Red roses of pain oozing
Red wine breaking roses through his skin,
The white roses of skin opening their sores.
The spirit, absorbed, must break out.
The season is full; all flowers open.

ii.

Do you believe anyone dies
Of drink? Little sister, big sister,
No. One dies of roses
That must be drunk from the river,
The roses of water, the roses of glaciers,
The blood of winter, the blood of father,
Christ, the blood of wine,
The blood of roses, to find,
Beyond roses, love, the pure light,
Spilled
Out of mother's hair it spilled,
Out of father's hands,
Out of sister's absence spilled

The pure light and broke
Into red, into green, into violet
Roses, violent roses, rising.

iii.

Remember the abandoned house,
The crystal chandelier,
The three-sided prisms
We plucked out of the ceiling
So we could roll the broken light
Over walls, over floors, over
Our faces, and our eyes
Could see the world as small,
Each distant object surrounded
By rainbows, we said, by beauty.
Now we know that it was broken
Light blooming its broken roses
That must be drunk
To return the roses of color
To the white light.

iv.

Our little brother, our dead brother,
Had brown roses in his eyes
That were so pure
They drank the whiteness itself
Until the roses of death
Slept around his face
And he was covered
With brown roses of earth

That drank
All colors out of his flesh
Until now, thirty-three years later,
Only the hard roses of bone
Remain.

v.

When the green grass is tired
Of catching the dark roses of the night,
Each of us must let
The lids of our eyes
Lock the roses of color
Within: without.
But brother, wait.
When fear threatens to drown you in a river,
Swim out of the wet roses of waters
That pull you,
Let the big and almost brutal
Roses of your hands
Open the sleeping roses of love.
They are small, but growing, brother.
Look!

Och kom och lek med mej.
Come and play with me.

THE BLUE DRESS

I will go to my mother's house.
A white-haired woman will come to the door.
She will hesitate, wait until a light
Will light her face.
Am I her sister? Her mother? Her daughter?
She will know I have been there before.
"Daughter, is it you? Come in.
Close the door. Close the door."

The doors in my mother's mind
Are closing, one by one.
She cannot remember my name.
She cannot remember the name of her son.
She cannot remember the color of his eyes.
My blue-eyed brother has been lost for years.
How will he ever be found, if his mother
Does not remember the color of his eyes,
If she does not remember his name,
Or mine?

How do I go to my mother's house
When even the light that occasionally lights
That last room
Is losing its shine?
Somewhere way back,
There was a new dress that was blue.
She remembers that dress. She wants one.

I buy her a new blue dress. What else
Can I do? A light flickers
In her eyes.
There is something about the color blue.

How do I go there,
And what will I do,
When all the rooms have closed, one by one,
And the blue dress is gone
With the color of my brother's eyes,
His name, and mine?
How do I go to my mother's house
To close her eyes
For that last time?

POEM FOR MY MOTHER

Remember when I draped
The ruffled cotton cape
Around your shoulders,
Turned off the lights
And stood behind your chair,
Brushing, brushing your hair.

The friction of the brush
In the dry air
Of that small inland town
Created stars that flew
As if God himself was there
In the small space
Between my hands and your hair.

Now we live on separate coasts
Of a foreign country.
A continent stretches between us.
You write of your illness,
Your fear of blindness.
You say you wake afraid
To open your eyes.

Mother, if some morning
You open your eyes to see
Daylight as a dark room around you,
I will drape a ruffled cotton cape
Around your shoulders
And stand behind your chair,
Brushing the stars out of your hair.

PEREGRINE FALCON

Only the female falcon is a true falcon.
She stalks her prey in the sky, folds
Her wings and plunges through the air.
In Audubon's picture, the female duck
Stretches her long neck back
As her heart is gorged.

Audubon was a realist. Even among men
It is not uncommon for the hunter to eat
The heart of his catch. The reason

Might be forgotten. I want to tell
My daughter I do not have the strength
Of a bear nor the grace of a deer.
I do not have the bravery attributed to
The Spanish soldiers whose hearts were
Eaten by the inhabitants of the New World.

I have faults. I love. I try to stay
Close to reeds, water. Daughter,
The distance between us strikes at my heart.

But I cannot question the peregrination,
Or which one of us is migrating. I cannot
Tell her that the hunger to control
The New World cannot be satisfied.
In this civilization, only the heart
That is given can be taken.

THE ROADS IN THAT TOWN
HAVE NO NAME
for Thom Tammaro

The roads in that town have no
names, and the houses no
numbers, yet everything is
predictable, until
a red truck turns
over in the ditch in front of
the white house where
I and my younger brother
were born.

If a truck
that is supposed to travel straight
down the road can flip
over on its side, or its back, the wheels
spinning, it might be able to jump up,
rear like a horse, lunge
like a mad dog, and come rolling
sideways to the place
where I stand.

I run up the green hill
where I rolled to get dizzy, up
the front steps where I
jumped, learning to count, across
the large verandah where I stood
and looked down the road,
naming things,
while adults sat in striped canvas chairs
sipping coffee

in the sun.
The glare off the white walls
almost blinds me,
as I pull at the front door
to get it open, wait in the dark
entrance for a moment, run up the darker
stairs, and into
my room.
There is a cramp

in my chest, and I have trouble
breathing. Suddenly I
remember
the sweet, sticky smell of
something being born – and I know
that there are great and
unpredictable powers.
Large trucks can be tossed,
like toys by a tired
child.

I catch my breath and walk.
over to something small that has
no name, pick it up, and
lay it, carefully, into
the tiny, red
bed my father has made
for my doll. Impossible things
are possible. And it is
all right.

ON SOME SUCH MORNING

On some such morning
when the lake is only reflection,
a boy will come down to the shore,
untie a small boat, climb in,
push out, and begin
to row.

Proud of his skill
he will let the oars fall
rhythmically, like wings,
as he moves out
across the clouds
leaving only the wake
that will still to be clouds
again.

On some such morning,
a man will come down to the lake
to see only some bird
breaking the reflection,
while he calls and keeps
calling,
as the morning turns to afternoon,
and afternoon
to evening.

On some such morning, afternoon,
or evening,

when doves call and keep
calling,
a man will be dreaming.
The woman beside him
will feel his eyelids
flutter,

and in her half-sleep
she will not know
if it is her own heart, that of
a bird, or some breast feathers
ruffling.
And she will turn. Her hand will fall
against his chest, where someone is
rowing, rhythmically,
and someone is

calling.

SAY IT HAS BEEN SNOWING

Say it has been snowing for days,
and just as the snow lets up
and the field is empty of even the tiniest tracks,
just then, when all that whiteness is untouched,
a voice says a word or a sentence, and

something walks out into that field.

You might be in a city,
or on a transcontinental flight,
but the animal whose name you heard
will walk across that field.

Say, then, that there is a whole geography,
inside you, of snowy fields, windswept deserts,
and quietly reflecting lakes,
and that you are the one who must choose
how the continent should be inhabited.

Sh. Before you open the book or turn on
the television, listen!

Are you ready?

It is snowing.

212

IN THE PLANETARIUM

And I lean back into the chair
as my mother must have
leaned back under the space
of my father's body.
A small light, a comet
approaches the sun.
My father's seed
approaches
my mother's. A soft laugh,
and I begin

to inhabit the space that grows
to hold me. Cells divide,
atoms spin
solar systems around me.
The comet's tail
is blown away from the sun.
My tail shrinks
in my mother's sea.
I grow fingers, toes. The arm
of the galaxy
will hold me

when I leave one space
for another
space.

SEVEN LETTERS TO ZACHARIAS
for Zacharias Topelius (1818-1898)

bewildered as a blown bird
my soul hovers and cannot find
foothold.

Sophocles

i. *Alkaid*

Zacharias, there are still Finlands
inside me, where white soldiers ski
until all colors have frozen
out of their eyes.
Trees whiten, birches,
and birds, ptarmigans.
Lakes carry them, snow-blinded.
And your heavens break open
Over this, our world
war.

ii. *Alkor/Mizar*

This is a difficult time,
Zacharias, my head
is full of contradictions, my body
is looking for a home. I think
about the molecules of flesh,
wondering what holds them
together, the skin, like the tension
in a drop of water.
My teeth, my nails.

And I break the skin
of the milk cooling in the pot,
cut out the eyes

of potatoes, slap the ears
of the kettle that burned me.
Even my comfortable shoes have turned
against me, their long tongues
– cut them off! –
arguing like fishwives.

Lo, the beasts
are restless. They want to eat
from the same trough, drink
from the same bucket, go paired
from the ark to a place
where they can
dance,
proud of their hunger, their grunts,
their fangs.

iii. *Alioth*

Zacharias, sometimes I wonder where
you are taking me.

There is so much space up there, to get lost,
to be confused by the lights on the dark
turnpike – my friend has vertigo, my mother
has vertigo, I am trying to keep my balance.
I am trying

to keep the lights in my eyes, as they say,
but some mornings they are dark nights
looking back from the mirror, and I, I know
about black holes where all disappears.

Zacharias, I have told others to write about
themselves through doors, stones, lampposts,
dandelions, but now I wonder what Cassiopeia

feels, being gone, herself, only her chair
remaining.

I dream about a white church in a white space.
I dream about an island, nebulous in fog.
I photograph. I hold a flashlight. Who
mentioned death? What are my hands doing?
And my arms, holding my hands?

iv. *Megrez*

Zacharias, I know I have not yet begun
to write the poems of the heavens.

I name the fish, the birds, the celestial
predators, trying to explain something

to myself, my son. The astronomers
named the dark places of the moon:

> Sea of Nectar
> Sea of Vapor
> Sea of Crisis
> Sea of Rain

Even when they knew it was waterless:

> Sea of Moisture
> Sea of Clouds
> Bay of Rainbows
> Seething Bay

As if, by naming, they could recreate a dream:

> Marsh of Sleep
> Lake of Dreams

Lake of Death
Seething Bay

But I don't even know what dream revolves
on the dark side of my skin

Or what lunar ocean I must name
in my belly's belly:

Sea of Serenity
Sea of Fertility
Sea of Tranquillity
Sea of Storm

v. *Phekda*

Zacharias, it is right that I address you,
whose recognition remains
within the borders of your language
and country.

Even the red horses
in the prophesies of your namesake
are running unnoticed.

During the day, our eyes can stop
at walls and trees, our words
can bounce off branches and crawl
up the wallpaper.

But at night,
when our vision slips through the glass
of the closed window
to land on cloud, moon, star,

there is no border between the dead

and the living.
You are as real

as my pillow, the man beside me,
the child in the next room,
the cat on the stair.

When the Arctic Circle drew its fence
around us, we were siblings
in the dark,
although a hundred years separated us.

Time and space being one, the years
slip away, and I drift closer to
your space, where molecules of our breath
already mingle with Einstein's, Newton's, Galileo's.

I can say the Milky Way is fact.
I can say the Milky Way is myth.
The doors of the hibiscus open.
Red horses are riding through the night.

vi. *Merak*

I have come to explore
the space behind
the undefined door, moving
the boulder of the intangible
to within my reach,
to scratch my hands,
five-feathered angels,
winged, bony, angular.

If I were looking for God,
I might have found him.
If I were looking for order,

system after system
would reveal itself.
Death is no question.
Love is already given.
But the exploration continues
until
the task will slip
into its own
simplicity.

I tell my friends the truth.
The skillfully turned phrase
lives, for the writer,
while it is being written.
The face of a child or a god or a lake
changes. It is that changing
that matters. Perfection
is a wall. If the poem is a goal,
allow me
to fail.

vii. *Dubhe*

Zacharias, day follows day.
I observe and write the changes
in the logbook of my sleep.

The spherical ship I stock for the journey
to terra terribilia
is filling up
with such ordinary things:
a thread, a needle, the blueprint
of a wing.

The question is:
How can I,

with the tools I gather on my walk
to the mailbox – odor of pine,
a fallen branch, the cardinal's
song – gather the heavens to me
and discern
in star explosion
the seed, the ocean?

Patchwork, little woman.
I paste my skin
to the inside of a sphere.
I stitch my son's face
to that of gardens.
I trace the bloodied paw,
my father's hunt, my mother's
crying, my brother's thirst,
my daughter's sex, my husband's
nightmares, riding, until
the empty spaces of the sphere
fill.

DOG DAYS

The farmers in Vermont
reach for guns in their sleep.

Mrs. Ketchum woke, one morning,
to a hundred dead sheep.

Which dog had gnawed
each gnawed-off face?

       Sirius
       is rising.

If a dog sleeps on your pillow
you will dream his dream.

My husband tosses in his sleep,
sleeping on my pillow.

Which act that I have forgotten
is he living in his dream?

The dog is waiting by Orion's feet.
It is hot. I am counting sheep.

FINDING THE ANDROMEDA NEBULA

i.

Start with the brightest star
in the square of Pegasus.

Follow the row of stars
running northeast
across the heavens, below
Cassiopeia.

That's Andromeda
chained to her rock.

Find the one star
that makes you question
your vision.

That's the Andromeda Nebula,
a hundred billion stars
spinning like a pinwheel,
so far away that the light you see
burned two million years ago.

ii.

I began to question my son's vision,
when he thought that any long-haired girl
rising from the sea
was
his sister.

He sees distant objects
cloudy as nebulae.
His eyes
are
what they are.

My vision is fine.
It can travel to the stars.
Gravity. Gravity.
Gravity keeps me chained
to the rock.

THE LYRE

Looking at the stars we find
the Dragon, the Serpent, the Lynx and
the Bear. You say:
Our solar system speeds
twelve miles per second
in the direction of
the Lyre.

For Orpheus is somewhere
singing.
The beasts of the sky
are tamed
and move like cattle going home
in the evening.
Everything follows: sun, earth, the stone
in the river.

Eurydice must have said:
"How do I tell him
not
to look back?"
For women want hands
to touch them
into song. But
Orpheus

looked back,
as I do,
as you do,
while the instrument of our playing
is flung into space
where it will drift,
pulling us.

224

CETUS, A LETTER FROM JONAH

The whales are singing.
They answer
each other.
They move
through the water
repeating
strange verses.
Listen, God.
Listen.

I would be frightened
if it were not
for the singing.
I move through a space
where Cetus,
at midnight,
is swimming
toward
Delphinus
singing.

NAMES AND TRAVELERS
OF THE MILKY WAY

Milky Way,
River of Heaven,
River of the Shepherd's Hut,
River of Nana,
Silver River,
Snake River,
River of Light,
Celestial River,

Cloud-eating Shark,
Great Serpent,
Bed of the Ganges,
Heavenly Girdle,
Ashy Path,
Path of the Ghosts,
Path of the Snake,
Path of the Chopped Straw Carriers,

Way of the Sun,
Woden's Way,
Birds' Way
Milk White Way,
Winter Street,
Women's Street,
Pilgrims' Road,
Mother of Stars,

The children are coming,
The souls are coming,
The doves are coming,
The ghosts are coming,
The giants are coming,
The heroes are coming,
The singers are coming,
The fishermen are coming,
The moon is coming,
The ostrich hunters are coming.

ALMAGEST, LAST LETTER TO ZACHARIAS

i.

When the synchrotron was being built
at Brookhaven National Laboratory,
I walked through the perfectly circular
underground structure
where particles would be accelerated
and split,
and I thought
of the mounds that were made
for some larger than human
eye,
and of their builders
who were named
after their constructions,
and of Pythagoras
who saw nature exposing
its precise mathematics
while things, according to
the second law, were moving
toward randomness,
and of Ptolemy of Alexandria
who made the most accurate
measurements of the earth
by using instruments devised
for the stars,
and of Gerard of Cremona,
who translated the Almagest,
where science had slept
for a thousand years,
and of the knowledge
that still sleeps
in the root of a word
or some old story's
metaphor,
and I knew it doesn't matter

whether the universe exists
without human perception
or not
for we can conceive of it as fractional
or whole,
the concept of heaven
can enter the human soul
and flow out like water
finding its own
level.

ii.

Like all who try to harness
chaos, with formulas and phrases,
I stand on the edge of the known world.
The smallest particle, the right side
of the brain, the region beyond
our galaxy is waiting.
The names I have used
as spells against the night
lead me to the word matter.
And like an alchemist, I juggle
the known elements,
not for gold, but for a unified
theory.

iii.

I sail out on the black waters
of the sound, the night speckled
with lights. Three miles from shore
I wonder if I can swim
the wave, the ray, the killer shark
home. I lie on my back on the deck
looking up.
And as the homing pigeon knows
by the slant of sunlight, the rotation
of stars, the magnetism of the earth,

how to find its way home,
the word sings through my bones,
is if they too were hollow.

iv.
The elements
fuse:
fire

with air
with the earth
floating in the water

of space
Space is
time

measured in distance
Dimension is
a matter

of perception
Change is
the only

constant
Conception
conceives

all
All is
relative

Mother
is the same word as
matter

230

v.

And a stranger in a restaurant
takes me
into the blue waters of
his eyes
to someplace inside
his brain, turning me upside down
like a face in a spoon,
turning me right side up, finding
my colors, the shape of my cheek,
to remember, or not remember,
not knowing I question where
I exist
in my body? in my brain?
in someone else's eyes
where I am tumbling?
Where am I tumbling?

vi.

Sh. Any one answer is no
answer. As the wheel
spun out animals and herbs,
genitals, skill and time,
and still spins,
the names of the ancient ones who found
answers
spin
with the remaining questions in
this pinwheel, whirlpool, circle
around the pole.

And like Vainamoinen, who went north
in search of the three runes
that hold the secret of absolute
origin,
I will travel north, in the sign of Gemini.

If the stars would be visible,
I would search for the twins
and name them Possible and Impossible.
But the night will be light.

And there,
where the invisible bear roams,
where the wolf I once created
with the shadow of my hands

walks, I too will walk
naming the impossibilities
that fetter the wolf:

> *the footfall of a cat*
> *the root of a rock*
> *the beard of a woman*
> *the breath of a fish*
> *the spittle of a bird*

to the present but invisible
stars.

LETTERS FROM THE ASTRONOMERS

If then the Astronomers, whereas they spice
A new-found Starre, their Opticks magnifie,
How brave are those, who with their Engine can
Bring man to heaven, and heaven again to man?
John Donne

I. *Letter from Nicholas Copernicus (1473-1543)*

The sun is the center of the universe.
The planets move around the sun.
Yesterday when I went riding,
it began to snow. The seasons
change. The earth
turns
on its axis.

Share these ideas with your
students,
but don't give them my name.
New continents are being
discovered.
Books are being printed. Witches
burn. I am afraid
of the spirit
of the times.
What will they do, if I say
the sun is the center of this cosmic
temple, if I say
its distance from the earth
is infinitesimal
compared to the distance
between the earth
and the stars?

I carry a pouch
of powdered unicorn's horn
and red sandalwood,
to cure
the ill. I have devised a new
monetary system.

I was asked to Rome to help create
a new calendar, but I declined.
My mathematics are not
sufficient. If you
have been trained in the art,
see if you can find the laws
that would prove
my ideas. Do you have a quadrant?
An armillary sphere? An astrolabe?

II. *Letter from Johannes Kepler (1571-1630)*

If we substitute the word "force"
for the word "soul," we shall have
the basic principle which lies at
the heart of my celestial physics.
                    Johannes Kepler

They say my mother is a witch.
She was arrested in the rectory.
They dragged her to prison in a trunk.
They want to put her on the rack.
For weeks she has been chained.
I am writing letters
asking them to release her.
My school has been closed.
The Protestant teachers have been burned
at the stake. My youngest child
died, of smallpox.
But I try to continue my exploration
of a celestial science.
I have derived a musical scale
for each planet, from variations
in their daily motions around the sun.
A five-note scale for Jupiter.
Fourteen notes for Mercury, and Venus,
repeating her one long note.
Such harmony. As I picture each planet
floating within the geometric perfections
of space, I think geometry was implanted in man
along with the image of God.
Geometry indeed is God.

III. *Letter from Galileo Galilei (1564-1642)*

They say I was arrogant.
Well, I was.
I had come far
from my father's numbers
and songs.
Before me, no one had seen
the moons of Jupiter,
the phases of Venus,
the mountains of the moon.

Now I am tired of arguing
with Jesuits and Aristotelians.
I have renounced my views
on the Copernican universe.
I have denounced my students
and friends. My book
is condemned. I cannot
put my mind at ease.
I have trouble

sleeping.
My daughter Virginia
reads the prescribed
penitential psalms.
What is Christianity
that it can be threatened?
The sun is turning on its axis.
I am old.
I am going blind.

IV. *Letter from Caroline Herschel (1750-1848)*

William is away, and I am minding
the heavens. I have discovered
eight new comets and three nebulae
never before seen by man,
and I am preparing an Index to
Flamsteed's Observations, together with
a catalogue of 560 stars omitted from
the British Catalogue, plus a list of errata
in that publication. William says

I have a way with numbers, so I handle
all the necessary reductions and
calculations. I also plan
every night's observation
schedule, for he says my intuition
helps me turn the telescope to discover
star cluster after star cluster.

I have helped him polish the mirrors
and lenses of our new telescope. It is
the largest in existence. Can you imagine
the thrill of turning it to some new
corner of the heavens to see
something never before seen
from earth? I actually like
that he is busy with the Royal Society
and his club, for when I finish my other work
I can spend all night sweeping
the heavens.

Sometimes when I am alone
in the dark, and the universe reveals

yet another secret, I say the names
of my long lost sisters, forgotten
in the books that record
our science –
        Aglaonice of Thessaly,
        Hyptia,
        Hildegard,
        Catherina Hevelius,
        Maria Agnesi
– as if the stars themselves could
remember. Did you know that Hildegard
proposed a heliocentric universe
300 years before Copernicus? That she
wrote of universal gravitation 500 years
before Newton? But who would listen
to her? She was just a nun, a woman.
What is our age, if that age was dark?

As for my name, it will also be
forgotten, but I am not accused
of being a sorceress, like Aglaonice,
and the Christians do not threaten to
drag me to church, to murder me, like they did
Hyptia of Alexandria, the eloquent young
woman who devised the instruments
used to accurately measure the position
and motion of

heavenly bodies.
However long we live, life is short, so I
work. And however important man becomes,
he is nothing compared to the stars.
There are secrets, dear sister, and it is
for us to reveal them. Your name, like mine,
is a song. Write soon.
                Caroline

V. *Letter from Albert Einstein (1879-1955)*

Yes, I have written
the President. I have told him
that if there is a nuclear war, the Fourth
World War will be fought
with sticks and stones.

Words do hurt me,
and there is no change in my heart
condition, but I am trying to complete
my unified field
theory. I cannot believe
that God is playing dice
with the world. The mystery
must be locked up
in the elemental infrastructures.

Forgive me for using
scrap paper. The other day
when my wife and I
were being shown
the huge reflecting telescope
at Mount Wilson observatory,
she asked why the instruments
were so large.

On being told
that they were trying to discern
the shape and makeup of the whole
universe, she said:
My husband does that
on the back
of an old
envelope.

239

ABOUT THE AUTHOR

Siv Cedering is the author of eighteen books, including two novels, six books for children, and several collections of poetry. Her writing has appeared in *Harper's*, *Ms.*, *Science*, *The New Republic*, *Paris Review*, *Partisan Review*, many other magazines and a hundred anthologies and text books including the reading programs of Harcourt Brace Jovanovich, Nelson Canada, Prentice Hall, Jostens Learning Corp., Natur & Kultur, Houghton Mifflin, Addison-Wesley, Scott Foresman, Education Queensland (Australia), and the Longman Group in London. Her previous collection of poetry, *Letters from the Floating World*, was published by the University of Pittsburgh Press.

Bilingual, Cedering has written half of her books in Swedish, half in English, and has translated books of poetry to and from both languages. She has illustrated four books for children with drawings and watercolors and a book of poetry with photographs. A self-taught writer, artist, and composer, she has received prizes and awards for fiction, poetry, screen-writing, and visual art, including fellowships for poetry and screenwriting from the New York Foundation for the Arts, a Best Book of the Year Award for her first novel, and a five year grant from the Swedish Writers Fund. Sven Nykvist has made a feature film based on a true story she developed in her Swedish Novel, *The Ox*. The film was one of the five nominees for the 1992 Academy Award for Best Foreign Language Film. She has done the narration, lyrics, music and illustrations for seven partially-animated TV programs based on one of her books for childrens. One woman shows of her paintings have been seen in galleries and museums from coast to coast, and she is working on her first exhibit of poetry sculptures.